Shrinking the SMIRCH

Jo Johnson

Illustrated by Lauren Densham

Published in 2014 by
Speechmark Publishing Ltd, Sunningdale House, Caldecotte Lake Business Park, Milton Keynes, MK7 8LF, UK
Tel: +44 (0) 1908 277177 Fax: +44 (0) 1908 278297
www.speechmark.net

002-5930/Printed in the United Kingdom by Hobbs
British Library Cataloguing in Publication Data
A catalogue record for this book is available from the British Library

ISBN 978 0 86388 996 7

Shrinking the SMIRCH

Jo Johnson

Illustrated by Lauren Densham

Acknowledgements

Many thanks to the following people who have spent many patient hours
reading and correcting countless smirch drafts. Your help has been invaluable in avoiding many mistakes before going to print!
Richard Johnson, Georgina Baker, Lee Rees and Ian Helmer.

Special thanks to Annabel Solomons who, despite having to manage a rather large smirch, has given so much time, encouragement and great quotes to the smirch project.

Also a huge thanks to the most delightful smirch shrinking cafe The Vintage Rose in Storrington, West Sussex. A great deal of the smirch has been created, corrected and consolidated in the warm interior of this fabulous cafe all whilst consuming the most delicious wares served by the most marvellous staff!!!

Contents

Introduction

What on earth is a smirch and from where has it come?

In 2008 the Multiple Sclerosis (MS) Society UK published a workbook called 'Shrinking the Monster'. The workbook asks the reader with MS to think about their symptoms as something external to them. There is evidence that this can be a useful way of taking a fresh look at troubling symptoms and managing the challenges long-term health conditions can create. Some people do this naturally. A well-known example would be when Winston Churchill referred to his depression as 'the black dog'.

What then is a smirch?

Many people contacted us to say they had used the ideas from 'Shrinking the Monster' with other physical or psychological health conditions.

The term 'monster' was used as a title for the original workbook but readers told us their 'monster' was represented by something much less dominant or tangible. Ideas people have shared with us include an animal, an intangible blob or even just a colour. We tried hard to think of something that would give people the freedom to create in their heads an image of whatever made sense rather than a monster that is associated with certain fixed ideas.

'Smirch' is another word for a smudge. We liked this word because it sounded a little less threatening than a monster. A 'smirch' is something that perhaps makes you feel your life is not as good as it could be.

Your 'smirch' may be a named physical condition such as MS, Parkinson's disease, encephalitis, epilepsy, chronic fatigue, fibromialgia, dementia, cancer or a stroke. It may be a named psychological diagnosis such as an eating disorder, anxiety or depression. Your smirch may even be someone else's diagnosis or a complicated bereavement. It may be a set of thoughts, feelings or symptoms that you have been troubled with for some time. Whatever your smirch, we hope that you will find this framework a useful way of managing your challenges. For many the smirch can't disappear but perhaps its power and control over your life can shrink.

Shrinking the Smirch is written in three parts. The first part helps you work out the impact your smirch has on you, what it makes you think feel and do. The second part asks you to create an image or description of your personal smirch and the challenges it gives. The final part describes 20 ways you can potentially shrink the power your smirch has on your life. You can use this workbook on your own or with your family and friends, or you might find it helpful to speak further to a specialist health professional about the ideas raised.

Quotes from readers of Shrinking the Monster

'It's a totally groundbreaking approach on Coping with MS.'

'Six months on it pops out but it's not rampaging as it was. Hurrah!'

'The workbook made me look at my symptoms in a different way.'

What this workbook does:

Provides an opportunity to think differently about your diagnosis or situation
We hope that this workbook might help you think about your challenges from a new perspective. This can be especially useful if people have lived with symptoms for a long time.

Uses psychological theories and models that have been proven to help people
Shrinking the Smirch is a novel approach, but it is based on psychological approaches that have been proven to work. This would include narrative therapy, cognitive behavioural therapy (CBT), acceptance and commitment therapy (ACT), visualisation and systemic-based approaches.

Focuses on changing how you think about your challenges and what you do
This framework is one that helps you to understand better what goes on in your head, body and life so that you can change the things that are within your control.

Makes sense to many people
Many people I have met tell me that they already think about their condition as separate from them. They talk about their condition as he, she or it. One lady told people the Queen of Sheba is visiting when her MS symptoms flared up; a man who had had a stroke described his weak side as 'Bill'; a lady with Parkinson's described her symptoms as 'Parky'.

> 'I would never have believed something like this could really help so much.'
> 'It's brilliant in making sense of things.'
> 'Makes wonderful sense! You'll see what I mean when you read it. Enjoy!'

Can be useful with children
Shrinking the smirch can be a useful way of talking about the challenges as a family. Children enjoy visualising and drawing and it can prevent all the difficulties being solely associated with the person with a given diagnosis.

> 'We drew some wonderful monsters and stuck them on the fridge.'
> 'My godchildren loved the idea of drawing "my monster".'
> 'My grandchildren have drawn what they think my monster looks like and we've had brilliant discussions.'

Puts you back in control
Many people who are living with a long-term condition feel they have no control over what is happening to them. This is perhaps not helped by some of the terms used for people such as a cancer victim, an MS sufferer, a disabled person rather than a person with a disability. It is hoped that the workbook will help you see that making small changes to the things you do control might make the impact of your smirch smaller.

> 'I just show it who's boss and it can either lump it or leave it. (For some reason it always just lumps it, never leaves, it's a stubborn so-and-so.'

What this workbook does not do:

Provide a magic answer
Any change of approach to managing life's challenges requires practice. If you learn, practise and use the strategies in the workbook you may be able to shrink the impact the smirch has on your life.

Eliminate the physical or psychological diagnosis
If you have been diagnosed with a physical or mental health condition, shrinking the smirch will not take away that diagnosis. The best it can do is help you think differently about your symptoms and recognise and change the things over which you do have control.

Belittle the problems
Shrinking the Smirch is a title that implies a light-hearted approach. This does not mean in any way that your diagnosis is not seen as serious, distressing and life changing. There is no intention in this book to belittle the huge challenges with which many of you have to live.

Imply you are the monster or the smirch!
Occasionally individuals have misunderstood the concept of the monster and felt the workbook implied that the person with the diagnosis is the monster. This is absolutely not the case.

Work for everyone
Some people will read the ideas in this workbook and think they do not make any sense. Everyone is different and some people will benefit from another approach. The reference section includes ideas from similar psychological models written in other ways so you can find a way of working with your difficulties that best suits you.

So let's get started

The quotes throughout this book have been shared by a panel of readers with various mental and physical health conditions, who are all working to shrink their own smirches.

Chapter 1: The Smirch Story

slimy

all the colours of the rainbow

FURRY OR HAIRY

crazy striped

different shapes

black & white

In a land far away

there lives a place full of creatures called smirches. Smirches come in many varieties. Some have spikes and just a few have tentacles like an octopus. Some smirches have faces, arms and legs with a definite human look. Other smirches resemble animals, whereas many don't look like anything that can be named, just a blob, a lump or a thing. Despite their many differences they share many common personality traits.

The key reason for living for a self-respecting smirch is to prevent humans from having any pleasure or meaning in their lives and to make them do things that will hurt themselves or other people. Smirches work hard to keep humans so caught up with their own thoughts that they can't enjoy the good things happening right in front of them.

They are not evil, just irritating little **fun sappers.**

Most of their time at smirch school is spent learning the Smirch Handbook. They have lessons to teach them to spot the distressed and how to use their tools to cause the most sadness and pain.

They each have a bag of accessories that they can use to achieve their aims. Old smirches have a large bag full of different pieces of equipment, whereas smaller ones have tiny bags with only one or two accessories. They are drawn to people who they know might be vulnerable to their ways. They know that a person will be an easier target if they have a heavy heart because something upsetting or traumatic has happened to them or if they are struggling to cope with life.

Most of the Smirches on the opposite page have been sent to us from real people! You can see some of them described in more detail in the "Smirch Yearbook" on pages 22 and 23.

Smirches are negative little creatures from birth, all inheriting the same key personal characteristics. If we were to view a smirch's CV, it might look a little like this:

SENIOR SMIRCH

PERSONAL INFORMATION

Address Bubbling Swamp, Smirchland   **DOB** 13 June 2002

PERSONAL CHARACTERISTICS

Accusing
Smirches want you to blame yourself for things that are not your fault. They like you to wonder why it is you they have chosen. They want you to fear they will pick on your children or grandchildren. They want you to dwell on why others can get rid of their smirches or have fewer symptoms. They like it when these fears overwhelm you and stop you doing anything that will make you feel better.

Self-absorbed
Smirches love themselves and are only happy when you are thinking about them and their place in your life. They love it when you ask questions such as: What will they do next? How will I keep them quiet? What if they get bigger or stronger? What would my friends think if they knew about my smirch?

Controlling
Smirches want you to believe they have total control of you. They want you to think you can only do what they allow. They want you to do things that will make you feel worse and to believe you can't do anything new or pleasurable in case it makes them bigger.

Unseen
Some smirches create symptoms that can be seen but many of the things they do are invisible to others. They cause panic, a blackness, fatigue, pain, a weak bladder, blurred vision, memory loss—symptoms that are difficult to bear but unseen. The smirches like that, so your pain is made worse by your fear that others will think there is nothing wrong with you.

Unpredictable
The smirches love it when you feel you have no idea what they will do next. They cheer when you cancel a holiday in case it's a bad week and they smile as you turn down an invite in case the smirch is having a strong day. They like you to feel they are not predictable in any way so that they stay in control.

ALLERGIES

Smirches have three serious allergies:

Allergic to the present
Smirches hate the here and now. They hate you to notice and enjoy what is actually going on. They want you to be worrying about the past, fearing the future and totally caught up in your head, remembering, planning, worrying and thinking. When you are fully involved in what is going on, they shudder with fear and break out in spots. They know they have no power in the present, so they must do all they can to pull you back into your head.

Allergic to kindness
Smirches also hate any act of kindness to yourself or others. They don't want you distracted from them by the needs of others and they want you to judge yourself harshly and then take out your bad feelings on those you love.

Allergic to words beginning with 'P'
Smirches detest many words beginning with P including planning, problem solving, pacing, prayer, purpose, peace, pleasure, patience, paper, play, people, popular and party.

KEY SMIRCH OBJECTIVES

- To stop you doing anything that is important to you or that will make you feel better.

- To prevent good relationships. Smirches know that it is easier to get your attention when you are alone.

- To exaggerate feelings of loss. Smirches know loss and grief cause great pain and that will give them options for boosting bad thoughts and feelings. They have no power over life or health but know bad feelings can make people do things that make them feel worse.

How smirches make you think

Smirch Handbook

Aims for thinking

Aim 1: Make sure humans spend as much time as possible tangled up in their thoughts and fears so they don't enjoy life.

Aim 2: Play lyrics and tunes constantly to distract them. Humans call these 'thoughts'.

Aim 3: Keep the human focusing on all the bad things that could happen in the future and all failures of the past.

Essential smirch equipment to impact thinking

Smirchigoggles

Invisible goggles to make the world and everything in it look rubbish—a rubbish body, a rubbish job—even closest family are not good enough when viewed by these glasses. They are so transparent that the humans don't notice the goggles are changing the view.

A Smirchipod

This very small device holds different tunes that are chosen to cause as much distress as possible. Common tunes include lyrics about the times you have failed, the people that have treated you unfairly, reminders of fearful situations, how life should be better, how you will not cope, how the future will be bleak and what other people think of you. Thoughts and worries are what human beings call these tunes and lyrics in their heads. All smirches can efficiently use a smirchipod.

Humans spend lots of time focusing on what is going on in their heads, as the saying goes 'with your head in the clouds', on autopilot. Thinking, worrying, planning, forgetting, panicking, worrying about panicking, fearing the future, regretting the past. Thoughts are just words and pictures in your head. We label them as fears, ideas, plans and attitudes, but they are just random words. Mostly they are not helpful words but unkind, guilt and fear-ridden words.

Smirches love the fact that you listen to the thoughts playing in your head, believing it all, as if it is a factual documentary on what has happened or what is going to happen in the future. They know that, if they throw in a picture, it will make you even more likely to listen to the words in your head.

They want you to listen harder to the lyrics they play so that you spend less time thinking about what's happening right now, what pleasures you are missing and the people around you who are important. When you are listening to their lyrics you are then not enjoying the film you are watching and you feel distant from the friend who is trying to talk to you.

'I felt a new feeling in my arm, the same tune started: "it is a new symptom, I am getting worse, I am going downhill, Mark will leave if I get any worse, I can't cope".'

Kate

Smirches know how easy it is to distract you with a thought:

A thought about your health or future to make you worry	A thought that you are not as good as others	A negative thought about your performance	What is someone else thinking about you?
'Not feeling good today, a relapse is coming.' 'It's getting worse.' 'What if he leaves?'	'Look how much thinner that person is.' 'Look at him.' He is so much more popular than you.'	'Well you messed that up.' 'Failed again.' 'Perhaps you will lose your job.'	'Did you see how he looked at you?' 'She thought you were an idiot.'

9

The smirches know that most of the time humans don't even notice the tunes that are playing in their heads or that they are listening to the lyrics as if they are true. Smirches find it strange that humans can't see that they are feeling upset, sad or angry because of the lyrics they are listening to, rather than what has actually happened.

They also know humans will try desperately to think more positively or distract themselves by exercising or working too much or withdrawing from others.

Sadly, it is hopeless. The words and pictures come back and the harder they try to get rid of them the louder the smirches turn up their smirchiplayers and then add some new lyrics like: 'See, you can't even get rid of your own bad thoughts and worries', 'you are a failure', 'your smirch is always going to win'.

Smirches just love the fact that such struggles take up SO much energy.

'My smirch is called "Gaucho" and is a slimy, unwanted presence in our life—something ugly and creeping that is always there, skulking in the background. Naming the monster? That is a great idea.'

'I came out of a meeting, my team were quieter than usual, the lyrics started playing: "I must have said something stupid, they all think I should have been made redundant, I am such an idiot, everyone prefers Gerry".'

Gary

$\mathcal{Y}$ou have heard the same lyrics time and time again but still keep listening to the popular tunes of

You are a failure.

You can't even keep a job.

Everyone will leave.

You will always fail.

What will people think?

Can you imagine what they will say?

It's not worth trying.

Stay in, give up.

No one likes you.

You are just not good enough.

Your pain is only getting worse.

This is the beginning of a bad phase or relapse.

How smirches make you feel

Smirch Handbook
Aims for feelings

Aim 1: Humans must be made to believe that all others are free of bad feelings.

Aim 2: Make humans believe that painful feelings are bad and avoidable and only happen to the weak.

Aim 3: Don't let the humans realise that the bad feelings are a result of the thoughts and pictures we play them.

Essential smirch equipment to impact feelings

This creates a strong physical reaction that makes the heart race, your blood pressures go up and your body perspire. This can make you feel shaky, weak or sick and even confused and often makes people feel like they want to run away or fight.

Adrenalin Pill

Smirchiscope

Makes you focus on small feelings and body sensations until the feelings and sensations are all you can think about.

Smirchinks

All smirches are given a set of syringes when they leave school to use with different coloured inks:
Red to make your blood boil.
Yellow to make you feel sick as your stomach churns.
Black to give a sense of doom and darkness.

Smirchiplayer

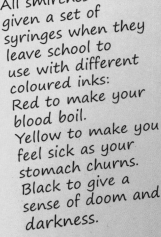

This plays moving films and clear images of things you would like to forget or your fears for the future. Smirches know that humans recognise what they play as memories or mental images. Smirches know that for the best impact this needs to be used together with a Smirchipod to create pictures and words at the same time.

Smirches need you to believe everyone else is happy and free of pain and negative emotions such as anger, sadness, fear and anxiety. Smirches play you images of other people's bodies, families, relationships, jobs and possessions. The images are airbrushed and they know to play you lots of tunes about your failures and lack of success coupled with images of a weak body, arguments and a bad, lonely future. They want you to feel that if only you had another job, new body or a different situation you would be free of all your bad feelings.

Imagine you have made a small mistake, you notice a new symptom, you remember a lost friend or a bad memory. Smirches rub their hands together because they know your brain will notice this minor problem before you do and will make your stomach lurch.

All the smirch has to do is play the right lyrics

Here it goes, starting again.

You are feeling bad.

Is it a relapse?

It can only get bigger.

Why always me?

You are so weak.

You will never be happy again.

This bad feeling quickly grows

Smirches know that, just like bad tunes, bad feelings have no power in themselves. Bad feelings are only a good tool for them to use because they know humans don't like bad feelings and it makes them start to struggle, worry and get caught up with their thoughts again.

Smirches know that humans believe they can push away or ignore bad feelings and that they try and hide their bad feelings from others. This makes the smirches smile; they know that mostly at this point they can sit back and giggle. They know that human nature doesn't allow bad feelings to disappear and they watch on as humans desperately struggle despite failing. The smirch watches as humans try and squash their bad feelings by drinking, eating or taking drugs, or distract themselves by getting busier, fitter or hurting others.

The smirch knows you are now totally controlled by how you feel and won't do anything again until you feel good.

As they wander away, it surprises them that such a good day for them started by just a small leg pain, one memory and a little disappointment.

'Tried to listen to my friend but could not, I felt so scared that the feeling in my arm was ominous, my heart was racing and I felt like I was going to pass out.'

Kate

'All I could think about all day was how rubbish I feel, felt so depressed and useless.'

Gary

'Feel like crying, my stomach feels like it's full of stones, the world feels dark. Feel really angry that no one understands or helps me. Feel really worried that I won't cope.'

Colin

What smirches make you do

Smirch Handbook

Aims for behaviour

Aim 1: Make sure humans don't get closer to who they would like to be or what they would like to do.

Aim 2: Make sure they hurt the people they want to have in their lives.

Aim 3: Make sure they do things that will add to their suffering.

Aim 4: Make sure they do lots of things to try and get rid of bad feelings.

Essential smirch equipment to impact behaviour

Urge Pill

So that you can't think of anything else but a certain urge. These urges are always negative and will take you further away from the life you want. The urge might be to overeat, drink too much, withdraw, shout at your family or harm yourself.

URGE PILLS

'I got home having felt terrible all day and had a row with my partner; she said I wasn't listening to her.'

Gary

'My friend went home but I couldn't really remember anything she said. I went to bed for the rest of the day.'

Kate

Smirches know the power starts with the thoughts, the lyrics; they know that soon the bad feelings will follow without them having to do much at all. Smirches know that, when the bad feelings come, another negative tune can be played and soon the chance of you doing something positive is less likely.

Smirches are masters at using all their skills together to make you behave in a way that you don't like. They love it when you feel so bad that you are easy to manipulate into doing what they want. They can then make your blood boil and quickly you are shouting at your friend, partner or children when it wasn't really their fault.

They love it when you start to feel so bad that you stay in and all the things you hoped to do now don't get done.

At this point they play you some of their favourite tunes

Oh what a failure you are.

There is no point in trying.

You have done it again.

You have spoilt it.

You are not good enough.

You are a bad person.

Everyone is laughing at you.

They are now happy, the negative circle is complete.

They can make you hear bad things and see unwanted images; they then know you will soon be feeling terrible. Then off you will go, doing things that they know take you further away from the life you want, and damage your physical and mental health.

Hooray, their job for the day is done. All the time their chosen human being is unable to do anything positive and won't experience any good feelings.

'I shout at her and tell her she is lazy and selfish, even though I know she can't help it. I have a few glasses of whisky and cancel my trip out.'

Colin

They can just leave them with a final tune or four

It's down, down, down.

Why do you even try?

Fail, fail, and fail.

You are just not good enough.

Smork

- Furry & changes colour.
- Lives in a cave.
- Makes me feel alone.

EQUIPMENT USED BY SPECIALIST SMIRCHES

The essential equipment that all smirches have has already been described. Specialist equipment that only some smirches have in their collection includes many other gadgets. Here is a list of ideas from other people that you might find helpful. However, no two smirches are the same, so your smirch will have many things that only you can understand.

Smirchivids The tiniest video cassettes that can be linked to the smirchiplayers. Only a few smirches have them. They are used with the right lyrics and images to create films and sounds to remind you of when something terrible happened. They can record their nasty little films so that when you see or hear things that are similar, your mind and body feel as if the real incident is happening again.

Generating machines These are a bit like a lottery gadget, but instead of throwing out numbers, throw out random words, smells or pictures. The words can be a label such as bad, depressive, MS, disabled, or the name of a person or place that has the power to remind of fears or events. Smells can be a familiar scent that arouses a powerful memory—pictures of a face, a bed, a stick or a baby. This works well with humans. The smirches know that just the right thing thrown out at the right time and place can draw things up into your head again and make you think and panic.

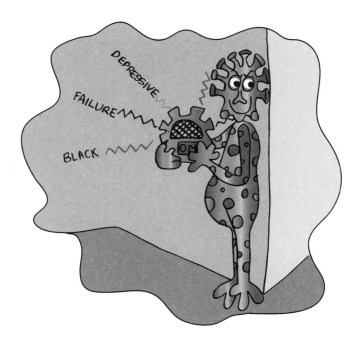

Vibrating coils Only a few smirches have coils; they are usually used on the hands, arms and head. They are made of thin clear wire so they can't be seen, but are wrapped tightly around the hand or arm. When the smirches blow on the wire the coil vibrates making the body shake or tremor.

BLOW HERE

Fatigue pipe This is a pipe that can be plugged into your finger when you are sleeping. People need a full tank of energy to deal with life. The fatigue pipe can be used to suck out your energy so that you wake up the next day with so little energy that even getting up feels draining and by mid-morning you are truly shattered.

MAXIMUM ENERGY

TIRED

FATIGUED

Claws Claws and brushes are used to brush and scratch limbs when people are not looking so that they then feel different sensations on their skin. It may feel like ants are crawling on you or that the area is numb or painful or like having pins and needles.

Paralysis spray This is a very rare purchase but occasionally smirches acquire a spray that can cause a part of the body completely or partially to lose the power to move. Some sprays create permanent paralysis, but sometimes the spray is weak and the body recovers in a few days or weeks.

Contact lenses These are daily contact lenses, but rather than making the world appear clearer they impair vision in some way. They can be used to cause double vision, blurred vision or make it hard for you to see the wood from the trees.

CONTACT LENSES

Brain smog A few smirches have brain smog and they can only use it on certain groups of humans, which they find very frustrating. The smog can be sprayed into the inner ears and it causes difficulties with clear thinking. Some smog is dark and creates lasting change, some smog is whiter and creates problems which come and go. The brain smog impacts different people in different ways. Some people experience changes in many mental abilities such as memory, concentration, thinking and learning. Others just have changes in one area such as speech or memory for words.

Panic button Most smirches know the buttons are best used with an adrenalin pill, some black ink and when smirchipods are on fast forward, so lyrics are jumbled and fast. As soon as the panic button is noticed, it makes a person feel overwhelmed by their symptoms, which usually makes them put up a fight, try and push away their symptoms, or avoid the situation they are in from then on. Smirches all know that if they can use panic buttons as much as possible people will soon be avoiding so many situations that their lives will shrink but the smirches' power will grow.

PANIC

You can look at the smirches described by other people but your smirch will be unique.

Think about your symptoms or diagnosis. What would your smirch be like if it really was separate from you, outside your body and mind? Give a face, shape, image or description to define your smirch.

What colour and pattern does it have?

Just one colour, stripes or spots?

What are its favourite tricks and accessories?

What does it look like?

Does it have animal features?
Does it look like a person?
Does it have ears? If so how many?
Does it have eyes? If so how many?
Are its eyes on stalks, on the back of the head or on its toes?

What does its voice sound like or is it silent?

What kind of bag does it have to carry its accessories: a sack, a carrier bag, a hand-made satchel?

What thoughts/lyrics do you often hear?

You are rubbish.
You will fail.
It won't work.
Stay in.
What are they thinking?
You are not good enough.
It's happening again.
They think I am weak.
No one likes me.
What will they say?
I am not a good parent.
Everyone else is better.
It can only get worse.
I am a burden.
People pity you.

MY SMIRCH

What would it feel like if you could touch it?

Is it slimy, spiky, smooth or rough?

What shape is it?

Is it tall?
Is it small?

What pictures and films does it always play?

Childhood memories.
The school bully.
The past failures.
Everyone else's happy life.
You sick and ill.
You in a wheelchair.
You gaining weight.

20

Draw your smirch here or write a description

'I think it should be called something like Fred or Dave. Don't know why. Either that or give it a funny name that makes you laugh when you say it.'

'I was amazed at how much better I felt after drawing my smirch. I suddenly felt in control of it, rather than the other way around. A bit like I'd won a game of hide and seek ... found you! You LOSE!!!'

Annabel

Name

Brief description

All the smirches shown here were given to the author by real people.

Slimeball

'A smirch that makes going out terrifying. It tells me I will fail again, people will stare, I will fall.'

Thinbee

An anorexic smirch
'It tells me I will be happy when I'm thin. It tells me I need to refuse food.'

Lassy

An anxiety smirch
'A rope (lasso) to make your body feel tight, red ink to make your head hot and a feather to tickle your tummy to make it feel jittery.'

Gregory

A bereavement smirch
'Reminds you of the happiness of others, sacks of tricks and radar watching for an opportunity to catch me when I might be ok just to drag me back down.'

Smoggy

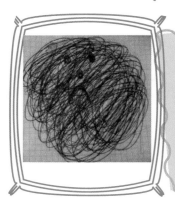

'This smirch affects me in many ways, I can see and feel it seeping through my veins, into my blood, muscles and heart. It makes me feel in pain or in a dark place of which I struggle to get out.'

Metal Micky Morton

'A multiple sclerosis smirch that is unpredictable and inflicts invisible pain that no one else can see or understand.'

Blackout

'My smirch has been around a long time but has been made bigger due to my brain injury. It is black, looks like death with cavernous eyes. It has a fatigue pipe, brain smog and a smirchipod with many tunes and a player with films of horrible things that have happened in my life. My ally is a care bear and when my death smirch plays its tunes, I sing the care bear song and then the smirch shrinks away and I can sleep.'

Jin

'"Jin", which is old English for genie, tries to grant my nightmares, lives in my dreams and subconscious until he wheedles his way into reality to make my life pure hell. He tells me I am not good enough, I don't deserve to be a mother and it's all my fault. He is always behind me. I feel his breath, but I know now that by turning around and staring him down he goes away, even if it's for a little while.'

The Wolf

'Into my mind popped a vision of a cartoon wolf with a sinister smile and salivating lips, dressed in a fedora hat and a raincoat, standing on a dark street corner under a dim light. After this, each time bad thoughts entered my mind I would see this smirch and was able to deflect my thoughts, even laughing at him.'

'Imagine a parasite that's a giant baby: lazy, childish, clever, selfish and has a set of its own feelings. It thinks it's the boss. It clings onto my back like a ride at the park bucking bronco, but it doesn't realise: it tires me, makes me feel mad, frustrated, dizzy and sick.'

'I try and remember the wolf smirch is a devious whatsit that changes tack when you're on to him and so I keep visualising him as the instigator of bad thoughts.'

So... do you feel ready?

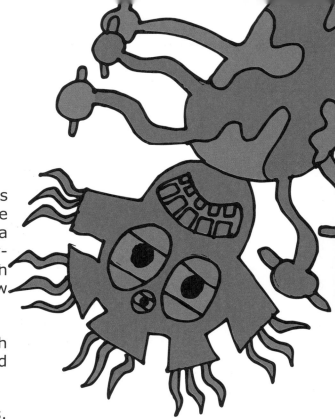

The smirch is going to be a life-long companion for many of you. If your smirch represents a neurological disease such as multiple sclerosis, Parkinson's disease, encephalitis, stroke or brain injury, these smirches will never leave your life. If your smirch represents a psychological diagnosis such as clinical depression, an eating disorder or an anxiety-based condition, the symptoms may always trouble you. Even if there are times when the smirch takes a holiday, you know he will be back when the going gets tough. Few smirches can be completely extinguished for ever.

If you are going to have a smirch in your life, can you find a way of relating to this smirch but not fighting and struggling with it? The fighting, trying to ignore it, pushing and shouting at it, takes energy which you could be using elsewhere.

In the last section we gave the smirches their credit; they can be quite influential creatures.

- Can you get your life closer to how you would like by shrinking the impact the smirch has on your life?

There is evidence that you can, whether old or young, healthy or unwell, with or without disabilities and whatever your history or future.

- Can you see that some of your pain and distress is due to the struggle you are having with the smirch?

- Can you see that there are perhaps small things that are in your control that you could change?

If your answer is 'yes', even if it is a small, pitiful, terrified, doubtful answer, you are ready to change the relationship you have with your smirch.

'I have actually been telling people for ages that, "I think I have Pixies—they think it's funny to creep in the middle of the night and swap my legs for somebody else's! I don't know whose legs I have on today but they're not mine...and they need a bit of a shave too...!"'

This will not make your smirch happy

The smirch was hoping you would see before you bought this book what a waste of time it was and put it back on the shelf. When you paid your money, it was hoping it would sit on your shelf with the other helpful books you have ignored.

The smirch is now getting more desperate so he has put on his smirchipod and is already playing you those old familiar tunes

This won't work.
You have disabilities, what can change that?
How ridiculous.
What will people think?
You are too weak.
I'll give it a week.
This is not for people as ill as you.
Nothing helps problems like yours.

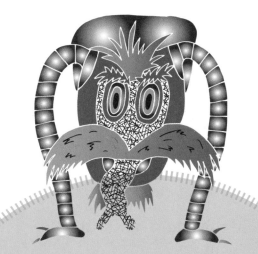

The smirch then slips on a film of

The time you tried to give up a bad habit.
Last night when you drank too much.
You under the duvet.
You shouting at your children.
A hospital bed.

Who is your smirch to you?

Have you a picture in your head of how this smirch looks and sounds?

Have you recognised how he makes you think, feel and what he makes you do?

Have you recognised his favourite pieces of equipment?

So, what sort of relationship do the two of you have?

Is your smirch

- a pet that can be tamed?

- a partner you wish you had not chosen?

- a naughty child who has never been taught how to behave?

- a weed that needs to be pulled out?

- a harsh teacher who is too strict?

- a new colleague who doesn't understand the way the team works yet?

- a wild animal like a wolf or a bear that needs to be caged?

- an unwanted neighbour who needs evicting?

'My smirch is a person trying to get out from a big black cave.'

'It looks a bit like a dark shadow just behind my right shoulder ... not sure why the right and not the left!'

What impact do you want to have on this smirch?

We are using the word SHRINK but you might want to use a different word that better suits how you imagine your smirch and the relationship you share.

What will you do with your smirch to lessen its impact on your life?

- Shrink
- Befriend
- Tame
- Train
- Dance with
- Discipline
- Reduce
- Minimalise
- Guide
- Negotiate
- Dilute
- Build a cage around
- Show him who is boss

Will you have an imaginary friend to support you?

It is very normal for children to have an imaginary friend to help them and give them support when they feel frightened or lonely. Some people find it helpful to imagine they have somebody or something on their side too. What will your supporter be like?

- A cuddly teddy bear that comes alive when needed?
- A perfect imaginary friend who makes no demands?
- A beautiful flower or tree that speaks kind words?
- A pet like a kitten or puppy that is warm?

Or someone else?

If you have a living faith in God, then He will be your supporter. Maybe you can think of a friend or family member and the things they would do and say in order to help you do the things that will shrink the smirch. If that person is still alive perhaps you can share your goals and plans with them in reality. Read more about all of this in 'Shrinking tip **17**, Ganging up on your smirch.'

Will you have any tools or gadgets to help you?

- A remote control that turns off the smirchipod and player?
- An antidote for his pills?
- A liquid to change the colour of his inks?
- A lead to control the smirch?
- A shield to defend you against the generating machine?

'I'd rather feel that I'm befriending and taming it.'

'It is a monster but my monster and so I have reclaimed it as just that. It's here, I don't like it and I wish it wasn't around but it is and I accept that and as long as it leaves me alone, we live in relative harmony.'

Chapter 3: Starting your Smirch Journey...

RESOURCES PACKED

EMPTY
EMPTY
EMPTY

20 ways to shrink your smirch

Aims for 'not shrinking' from the Smirch Handbook

Aim 1

Keep from humans the following 'two essential truths' if you don't want your powers to be diluted:

Truth 1

Their thinking, feelings and actions are very closely linked. Humans don't seem to realise that what they think makes a big difference to how they feel and then that changes what they do, which changes how they think, and the loop goes on for ever. This loop is a smirch's best friend; if the humans start to see clearly, they notice the lyrics we are playing and ignore them.

Truth 2

Their brains are created in a way that makes them unique. Humans love their pets so much that they think that their brains function in the same way. Animals are creatures of habit, destined to be stuck in their ways. The job of the smirch is to make sure that the humans don't realise that they have a unique ability to think in a much more flexible, creative and rational manner and can learn new ways. Keep them thinking they are much like their pets who, despite having some good basic skills, can't have faith, show respect, change the way they act or show kindness to self and others in order to make their health and relationships better.

Aim 2

Keep them alone for as much time as possible.

Humans are social beings; they are much happier and healthier when they spend time with others. This is not good for smirches as the humans get distracted and are less easily pulled into their thoughts by our tunes. Do anything you can to make them stay on their own, hide under the duvet, pretend they are ok or give up jobs or hobbies. Then they are guaranteed to stay unwell and stuck in their own destructive cycles.

Aim 3

Prevent them from hearing about any research that might help them improve their mental or physical well-being.

The senior smirches try and read all the scientific research so they can hide what makes humans stay well, mentally and physically. Smirches can then use this information to make humans do the exact opposite.

Your resource bag

If your smirch has equipment, it is only fair that you too have a full bag of resources to shrink your smirch. You might want to draw a resource bag that you can imagine holding all your tips and techniques that work to shrink your smirch.

As you progress through this workbook you will read about different skills to put in your resource bag. You might like some of the ideas but others won't match what you need. Some skills will be useful some of the time but at other times they won't work.

As you become aware of your smirch and his games, you will get better at noticing what is making life difficult and knowing what works best and in which situations.

In this workbook you will find 'leaked' research alerts, from a recent raid on smirch headquarters.

You can be assured that what the smirches were hiding will work in your best interests, so take note.

Draw your resource bag here

RESEARCH ALERT

CONFIDENTIAL
TOP SECRET
CONFIDENTIAL

Shrinking tip 1
Decide who you want to be and where you want to go

Would you

start a journey without thinking about where you would like to go and how you are going to get there? Have you ever thought about what you really want to be like? School, parents and society give us a lot of messages about what we **should** be like. They say you must be: thin, happy, in love, married, a parent, rich, clever etc. Smirches have a field day pointing out how we are fat, poor, lonely and a failure.

> **This excerpt from The Message version of the Bible gives a good summary of what most of us would like our values to be. This is read at lots of wedding services (1 Corinthians 13).**
>
> *'Love never gives up.*
> *Love cares more for others than for self.*
> *Love doesn't want what it doesn't have.*
> *Love doesn't boast, doesn't have a big head, doesn't force itself on others, isn't always "me first," doesn't fly off the handle, doesn't keep score of the wrongs of others, doesn't revel when others grovel, takes pleasure in the flowering of truth, puts up with anything, trusts God always, always looks for the best, never looks back,*
> *but keeps going to the end.'*

This is a tough benchmark and you certainly need divine intervention to live like that but it is a great starting point for thinking about what are your values. Everyone is different but most people would probably want to be described as honest, friendly, kind, generous, a supportive partner, a good friend or a loving parent.

Decide who you want to be and what your true values are. Values are not

goals. Goals are things you can tick off as finished such as getting married or buying a house. Goals are important but values are different; they are what you want to be like as a person.

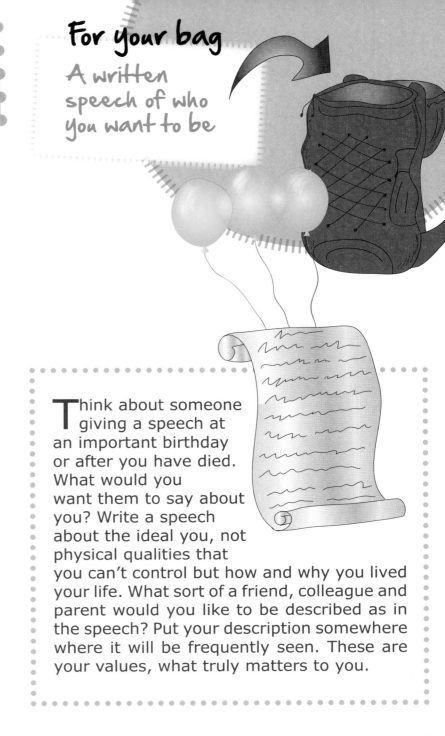

For your bag
A written speech of who you want to be

Think about someone giving a speech at an important birthday or after you have died. What would you want them to say about you? Write a speech about the ideal you, not physical qualities that you can't control but how and why you lived your life. What sort of a friend, colleague and parent would you like to be described as in the speech? Put your description somewhere where it will be frequently seen. These are your values, what truly matters to you.

These smirches love to make you go against your values; they love it when you are unkind, impatient, angry, self-absorbed and when you give up.

Smirches love it when they trap you into doing the opposite of what you want to do. They play their top tunes to make you feel bad until you do something unhealthy or that will upset others. Smirches know that they have the upper hand all the time you don't realise their tunes are linked to what you do.

Smirches know that people think they are trapped in their habits, they know they listen hard to the tunes in their head: 'you can't change, you always do it that way, nothing works'.

They think: 'I play this tune, he feels bad, off he goes to the bottle.' 'I play this tune, she feels scared, goes to bed.' 'I play this tune, he feels angry, shouts at his wife.'

So first decide what truly matters to you and what sort of person you want to be.

Then start noticing what you are doing and how events, thoughts and feelings are linked.

Notice when your behaviour fits with how you want to be: a kind word to a friend, a healthy walk, a rest or treat, and when what you are doing is the opposite to how you want to be: over-indulging in food, withdrawing or shouting at your family.

Ask yourself three questions:

1. What am I doing too much?
2. What am I not doing enough?
3. Where do I want to be?

Each section of this workbook will give you more ideas of things you might want to do more or less of in order to shrink your smirch.

RESEARCH ALERT

CONFIDENTIAL TOP SECRET CONFIDENTIAL

People who are gloomy and negative in outlook make those around them feel the same.

Shrinking tip 2
Decide how you are going to get there

For your bag

SMART goal sheet or section for SMART goals in your journal

SMART goal sheet

Date started : 7th October
Specific Goal To walk to work every day for five weeks
When to achieve by: 11th November

Walk to work every day for five weeks.

	M	T	W	T	F	S	S
	✔	✔	✔	✔	✔		
	✔	✔					

So you can now think about setting goals to take you in the right direction. Most sections in this workbook will suggest you set a goal.

The mistake people often make is they don't set **SMART** goals and fail, and then the smirches can quickly discourage. Make sure any goals you set are:

Specific
Measurable
Adaptive
Realistic
Time bound

Specific The goal needs to be so clear that anyone reading it could understand and do it, eg 'I will walk to work every Monday'.

Measurable The goal should allow you to measure how well you are doing, eg 'I walked to work every Monday for five weeks'.

Adaptive The goal needs to take you closer to who you want to be. Your goal will improve your health or relationships and make the smirch smaller, eg 'More walking will help fatigue and mood'.

Realistic Is it reasonable for you? Do you have all the physical, mental and financial resources you need to succeed? Eg don't join an expensive gym you can't pay for or set yourself goals that are too high for you at the moment.

Time bound Set a time, day and date when you will work on your goal, set start and finish dates or times. Only set goals for six weeks or less at a time, eg 'I will walk to work every Monday for four weeks starting on 6 January'.

Before you start

Do three things to make your goal smirch proof.

1 Think about all the possible reasons you won't succeed

For example: 'It keeps raining on a Monday', 'I have no decent shoes', 'I will be late for work', 'My boyfriend will say it's pointless'. Think about the solutions before you even start so you can be really sure you will succeed.

2 Focus on the benefits if you do succeed

'I will feel less tired, I will be fitter and my mood will improve.'

3 Tell someone about your goal

Smirches prefer secrets so that you have only their lyrics to influence you.

Bigger goals might need to be broken down into smaller steps.

If you don't succeed
...notice what happened and what lyrics the smirch played you to stop you starting or to remind you of your lack of success. Check your goal was SMART, take some deep breaths and start again.

RESEARCH ALERT

CONFIDENTIAL TOP SECRET CONFIDENTIAL

If you tell others your goals, you are more likely to succeed.

Shrinking tip 3
Start a 'Shrink the Smirch' journal

All smirches are predictable some of the time.

Have a good look and you will start to see patterns. Your smirch will have different routines from other smirches and they may change their pattern each season or every few months, but some of their behaviours stay the same. They worry that you will notice their patterns as their power comes from your fear that they are unpredictable. They know that if you start noticing, you might be able to catch them out and their control will shrink.

You might notice when you work with a certain person that you feel low. Going out to the supermarket might result in the stomach churning.

Perhaps the smirchipod gets turned up when you drive past a certain road or get spoken to in a certain way. Start to notice the patterns and write them in your journal.

For your bag

A colourful file, notebook or journal

'What a difference smirch-fighting has had! 'Bob' came at lunchtime and my eyes welled up. I realised I didn't have to listen to Bob or let him upset me. So he went away all by himself.'

Smoggle
Tues 5th Oct
Smoggle is black and white with yellow spots and lots of spiky hair. He loves using his claw brush to make my skin feel really horrible sensations. He also loves to remind me of the time when I felt really scared and couldn't leave the house. I knew he was nearby today with his generating machine because I started to feel really scared and anxious.

Notice the most frequent lyrics and in what situations they start playing. Notice how your body feels physically and how you feel emotionally, what sort of mood are you in.

A journal will help you get to know your smirch better and so stop him in his tracks. It will also help you get rid of all the thoughts and feelings that the smirch might have exposed you to. So journals have double shrinking power. In a journal you don't have to fear being judged or need to find the right words.

Notice each day how big or small the smirch is (give him a score of 0–10) and think what tricks have been used.

This workbook suggests many different areas of life to notice in your journal. When you have kept a journal for a few months, look for the patterns. Hormonal cycles might be important, or seasons, the weather, certain places and people, tiredness, hunger, alcohol, medication, over-activity or under-activity.

Once you have all this information you will be well prepared to shrink your smirch as you see the activities, people and times when he has the upper hand. Smirches thrive when you are unaware of the times that they are strong and you are vulnerable. The more information you have, the more you notice and make sense of their patterns, the smaller their impact will be on your life.

Have a section in your journal for recording SMART goals to change the things that are in your control. Record your progress in your journal and reward yourself for even tiny steps in the right direction.

Practice Ideas

Notice the fountains and the drains, the people and activities that make you feel drained of energy (drains) and the people and things that make you feel refreshed (fountains). Look at each thing you do and mark with an F for fountain, D for drain or N for neither.

Chapter 4: Essential Shrinking Tips...

The next four shrinking tips are vital shrinking skills to put in your resource bag and should be useful to everyone. These are:

- **Noticing (N)**
- **Belly breaths (B)**
- **Stabilising (S)**
- **Connecting (C)**

The first letter of each word gives the acronym **NBSC** so perhaps that could stand for a personal message to your smirch.

Now

be small, COWARD!

Shrinking tip 4 Start noticing

For your bag

A cheerful pen to write down times when you notice things

The smirches thrive by getting on with their tricks unnoticed.

As soon as you look carefully at what these smirches are actually doing rather than what you fear they could do, they immediately get less scary and powerful: they skulk off and hide, as they like to stay invisible.

Once you realise you don't have to fight with it, ignore it or hide from it, you can find some ways to just live with it. The energy you save can be used to do things that will make you as healthy as you can be and your relationships as good as possible.

The smirches have you so deceived that you don't see what they are up to. So noticing is the first step to changing the old habits and getting closer to the values you have chosen as important for you.

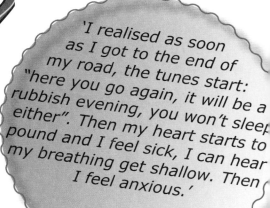

'I realised as soon as I got to the end of my road, the tunes start: "here you go again, it will be a rubbish evening, you won't sleep either". Then my heart starts to pound and I feel sick, I can hear my breathing get shallow. Then I feel anxious.'

Colin

Notice the loop, the tunes they play, the feelings that come and how this cycle ends up with you doing something that isn't how you want to be. Then the smirches cheer and another tune comes, 'see you will never change, you have failed, give up.'

Can you start to see that the tunes they play in your head as thoughts have the power to change how your body feels and then how you feel emotionally? Can you start to notice what you do in certain situations, when you feel anxious, when you are in pain, when someone upsets you?

Can you start to recognise when they have hooked you back in your head with a familiar lyric, a scary picture or a bad memory? If you can notice throughout the day when you are really enjoying what is going on rather than being entangled in your head, this will be a massive step forward.

If the smirch that lives with you

... is quite small it may be possible to get rid of it by simply starting to notice what it gets up to and getting on with your life.

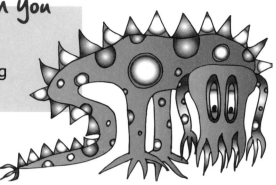

Smirches like a big impact so if they are not getting it, they may go off and find someone else to bother.

Bigger smirches won't ever go away but you can still learn to live in a way that shrinks their impact on your life. You have probably spent many years not really paying full attention to what you are doing. Noticing will take practice. Choose certain times during the day really to notice what you are doing, what you can see, hear, touch and feel, and really focus on experiencing whatever you are doing. Set an alarm on your mobile to prompt you to stop and notice at least three times a day.

Perhaps start with when you wake up: noticing for just a few minutes your first thoughts, the sound of the alarm, the feel of your body, the smell of your pillow. Pretend you have never been there, notice things you have not thought about before. Practise noticing the same sorts of things at different times in the day: before you eat lunch, when you clean your teeth. See if each day you can increase the amount of minutes you are actually savouring the moment.

There will be much more about noticing as we get shrinking.

'I now notice how ridiculously often I allow myself to wallow in a negative imaginary world and how readily I believe negative ideas about my past, present and especially my future. Just being aware of this and the different tricks my smirch uses has helped me to nip in the bud these negative thoughts before I start to feel anxious or down. Why make yourself feel bad due to your own imagination?'

Annabel

Practice Ideas

Get better at noticing by:

- Drawing an object and paying attention to all the small details you have never noticed, put in more and more details.

- Pretending you are a camera which needs to focus its lens on all the details of this experience and must include all you can see, smell, hear and touch.

- At the end of each day write a detailed account of at least one activity as if you were going to be cross-examined on every detail.

Shrinking tip 5 Belly breaths

Belly breaths are an essential tool that will help you shrink this smirch.

You might think breathing is easy because you have been doing it all your life, but many people are breathing badly which is making them feel stressed. You might actually be taking short shallow breaths, a bit like a dog panting. (Remember, we should not aim to be like our pets!)

Smirches know that shallow breathing causes a lack of fresh air; this is good for them as they know shallow breathing easily becomes a habit and keeps people feeling stressed. In order to feel calm you need to give your body and brain enough oxygen by 'belly breathing'.

Belly breathing is when you breathe in slowly and deeply, your belly should move out and you might feel your clothes tightening if you are doing this properly. This is a great tool to fight the smirches. Belly breathing makes them run and hide; they find it exhausting to watch! It will help you if you can improve your breathing at all times, but it will help especially when the smirches' tunes or your feelings make you feel overwhelmed.

Take time throughout your day to notice your breathing and, if it is fast and shallow, take a few minutes to do ten belly breaths. To learn any new skill the brain needs lots of practice until it becomes automatic and the old habits disappear. Few people can get on a bike, learn the piano or a new language in a few hours.

Belly breaths are the same, you have to practise.

**BELLY BREATHS
(diaphragmatic breathing)**

Practise this at least twice a day. Breathe in slowly and deeply through your nose into the bottom of your lungs as deeply as you can. Pause for a moment. Breathe out slowly through your mouth. Allow your body to relax. Repeat this so you do a set of ten. Keep your breathing slow and even. Don't gulp in a big breath or let out your breath too quickly. If you can do this for five minutes twice a day, you will notice a reduction in anxiety and feelings of stress within a couple of weeks.

For your bag
Pictures of lungs in various places to remind you to practise your belly breaths

'I realised that I am panting like a dog most of the day, I also realised it is often when I am caught up with my thoughts, my smirchie tunes playing loudly. At first I found belly breaths (I think the correct term is diaphragmatic breathing) really hard. I was determined to give it a go and after a few weeks of practising in the car, in the shower and before I went to bed I found I could do it easily. Now when the smirchie tunes come on, I can quickly take a few belly breaths wherever I am and it does help me feel more able to cope. Although on some bad days I have to do it fifty times!'

Colin

Shrinking tip 6 Stabilising

Psychologists use lots of different terms to describe the ability to stabilise or calm yourself when things feel overwhelming.

I like the phrase 'drop an anchor'. It hints of making yourself more stable in the emotional storm. In urban slang the same term is used to stand on the ground after you have fallen down drunk!

This is a skill that helps when you feel unable to cope and overwhelmed by the rush of thoughts, emotions or bad memories.

Stabilising or 'dropping the anchor' puts together belly breaths with noticing, really focusing on what is in front of you.

'I have always struggled to cope when my feelings come suddenly like a massive wave. I feel sick, panicky, ill and generally end up sleeping. I have been practising making myself feel better by using the drop an anchor. I am amazed as for me it helped first time. I have been practising lots and for the first time I have not been to bed in the day for a week.'

Kate

For your bag

'Drop an anchor' technique

DROP an ANCHOR

- **Push** your feet hard on the floor and straighten your spine.
- **Take** a deep slow belly breath as you count to four.
- **Notice** your stomach pushing out, your waistband getting tighter.
- **Breathe** out as you count to four.
- **Look** around and notice five things you can hear.
- **Imagine** a moment of pleasure like how the sun feels on your skin when you walk off a plane or a cold drink after a long walk.
- **Take** another deep breath as you count to four.
- **Notice** your stomach pushing out.
- **Breathe** out.
- **Notice** what you can see and what you are doing and focus on the here and now.

So you have some useful things in your resource bag. Can you see your smirch shrinking already?

He will probably already be planting some lyrics in your thoughts: 'this won't work, see you tried it and it doesn't, don't bother with the practice, it will be pointless, give up on this weird rubbish now'.

Shrinking tip 7 Connecting

Connecting with whatever you are doing is the opposite of being on autopilot or having your head in the clouds.

Connecting is really noticing and focusing on what you can see, smell, hear and touch around you at this moment. People around you will feel you are listening and giving them your full attention.

Some people call this 'mindfulness': instead of having your mind full of all the things going on in your head, you are aware of what is happening around you.

Connection or mindfulness is actually **SO simple** but also SO hard. The more you start to notice whether or not you are on autopilot or connected to the real world, you will see how easy it is for the smirch to hook you with a timely lyric or picture.

Connecting is a skill that in a busy world we have lost. Children are much better at it. If you watch younger children they are mostly fully immersed in what they are doing and much happier for it. Watch a small child looking at an insect or when it snows or a rainbow appears.

RESEARCH ALERT

CONFIDENTIAL TOP SECRET CONFIDENTIAL

Regular connection practice improves sleep, mood and anxiety. Minds like bodies become healthier if exercised in the right way.

RESEARCH ALERT

CONFIDENTIAL TOP SECRET CONFIDENTIAL

After just eight weeks of practising connection every day for at least ten minutes, positive changes in the parts of the brain that control emotions could be seen.

Smirches know that if people start connecting to what is happening, their relationships get better and their mental and physical health does too. If you are really aware of what you are doing, you will enjoy it, and be much less likely to crash the car, shout, make a mistake, over-eat, binge drink or be overcome with your fears or mood.

Connecting is a skill that most people find hard to learn. It is just about noticing when the smirch has dragged you back into your thoughts, then learning to parachute yourself back onto the ground.

You will need to practise connecting or savouring the moment several times a day and no one will ever be able to perfect it.

'I decided to really try and connect every time I walked my son to school. The first time I did it, it was SO hard. I kept getting distracted by what I had to do at home and realised I had not heard anything the poor little chap had said. Each week I have got a little better. We have even been practising together. He says, 'look at the colour of the trees Mummy and listen to the leaves crunch under our feet.' I feel like I am enjoying this half an hour so much more.'

Kate

Practice Ideas

When eating, really savour the taste and smells. Notice that just seeing the food makes your mouth water. Slow your eating to appreciate the experience.

When walking, really notice the way your body feels, what it feels like to lift your arms and legs as they move. What is the sound of your feet on the path?

Give yourself spot checks at set intervals in the day. Notice what is going on in your thoughts; how are you feeling, what is your body doing and feeling like, what is happening in the world in front of you?

For more practice put mindfulness or connection exercises into a search engine and you will find more ideas.

Chapter 5: Thinking, Feeling and Doing

Smirches are very good at playing you thoughts that tempt you to tune in.

The smirches are well aware that if you don't notice what you are doing you become more vulnerable to their tricks and more likely to upset people, have accidents and do things that will make you less healthy. So you need to become more aware of the 'thinking, feeling, doing cycle'.

'Your mind is the garden, your thoughts are the seeds, the harvest can either be flowers or weeds.'

William Wordsworth

Shrinking tip 8
Getting your head out of the clouds

Some psychologists use the term 'fusion'.

This refers to the times you are so caught up in your thoughts that you and what is playing in your head have become inseparable. This is a bit like living with a bag over your head.

If you had a thick cloth bag on your head, how good would your conversations be? How much could you enjoy a book or a film or a walk in the fields?

This is how life is when you are focusing on the smirch tunes and films all day—you are missing your life.

You can ignore what your smirch is saying or fight with it, but the struggle takes up so much energy that you might as well have a bag on your head!

For your bag
A list of the smirchs' top five tunes and some untangling techniques

SMIRCHIPOD

Smirchs' top 5 Tunes

'You are rubbish.'
'Don't leave the house.'
'Nobody likes you.'
'Why even try?'
'Give up now.'

CONFIDENTIAL
TOP SECRET
CONFIDENTIAL

RESEARCH ALERT

A negative thinking style reduces life expectancy.

So you need to add to your resource bag

Ways of getting untangled or defused (the opposite of fusion) from the tunes and lyrics of our thoughts.

> **The next set of skills for your resource bag are:**
>
> - **More noticing**
> - **Recognising** the tunes
> - **Untangling** techniques

Noticing

Sometimes it is enough to notice you have been pulled back into your head and then you can have a fresh look at what is actually happening right now. Start to notice throughout the day: are you there or in your head? If you are in your head, what tunes are playing? We all have our favourites.

Why me?

I am a rubbish partner.

If only I had a better...

I am not as good as others.

It's just not fair.

Recognising

There used to be a TV quiz called 'Name that Tune'. A few notes of a tune would be played and the contestants would have to guess the song. Sometimes the smirch tunes are like a popular song: once it gets into your head it plays and plays. That's when **you** have to play **'Name that Tune'.**

Can you label the type of thinking you are doing? Is it planning, worrying, fearing, daydreaming, boiling in anger, resenting? Say to yourself: 'The smirch tune has got me worrying'. Then see if you can name the song. You will have a favourite few that appear time and time again: 'My rubbish job', 'Why am I treated like this?' 'The difficult relative', 'The spiral into death or disability'.

Sometimes that will be enough
'Ha! I caught out that smirch playing its favourite song again!' You can then make an attempt to get back to paying proper attention to what you are doing.

At other times you will need to work harder
at getting rid of the tunes. Remember that these are just words and pictures in your head that are normal and unavoidable but mostly are not helpful or truthful.

Untangling

Here are a few untangling techniques to manage your thoughts. Try them all and see which ones work.

First work out what the key thought is:

- I am a bad mum.
- I am rubbish at my job.
- I am stupid.
- I will fail.
- I am getting worse.
- It is the beginning of a bad phase.

 Imagine a panel of sensible people.
They have to decide if the key thought is the truth. Would they have any evidence against you? What is the evidence for and against?

Am I stupid?

'I have a degree. People tell me my ideas are good. I have just been promoted. I have just made one mistake.'

The verdict: I am not stupid.

Am I a bad mum?

'I forgot it was swimming day and then shouted at her. Everyone shouts sometimes, I love her dearly, I spend lots of time, reading and playing with her. She was disorganised and I over-reacted. I apologised and gave her a hug.'

The verdict: I am a good mum.

 Imagine the smirch is like a parrot on your shoulder or a school bully. Would you put up with that in real life? Someone constantly berating you as stupid, rubbish, not good enough?

 Imagine the thought or tune being **sung in a silly tune** or as a nursery rhyme.

 Imagine the thought is coming from a **cartoon character** such as Bart Simpson or Bugs Bunny.

 Imagine you are **reading it as a headline** in a newspaper that you don't respect or believe the content.

 Recognise it for what it is. **The smirch is playing me the lyrics of** 'I am stupid' or 'I am having the thought that I am a bad mum'.

 Imagine your thoughts and images made into a **radio programme** or played to your best friend. What would others say?

 Do a **different mental task,** eg count as many nursery rhymes as you can, count back in sevens, name everything in one room in your house.

Work out when your thoughts are most often in the clouds, when you are most likely to get hooked. Think about if you can **change the sequence.** If it is when you wake up, get up straight away; if it is when you drive past an old place of work, choose another route.

These techniques take practice.

First you just need to start noticing when the smirch pulls you into your head. As you practise you will get quicker at coming back into the present moment and feel mentally much better for it. The smirches know that the easiest way to keep people mentally unwell is to make them spend as much time as possible listening to their tunes and watching their movies.

'My partner pointed out to me that I was not watching the TV programme I had asked to put on. I realised I had got caught up in my head again. I found it really hard to watch the programme but I am noticing when I start listening to the smirchipods.'

Mary

'Every morning I lie and analyse bad things and whimper at my weakness. However this morning was different as into my mind popped a vision of a cartoon wolf with sinister smile and salivating lips, dressed in fedora hat and raincoat standing on a dark street corner under a dim light. After this, each time bad thoughts entered my mind I would see this smirch and was able to deflect my thoughts, even laughing at him.'

Ian

When you have noticed you have been pulled into your head, you can picture yourself taking off the bag or coming out of the clouds and parachuting back into your life.

Pretend you are someone arriving from a new planet. What can you see? Notice the colours and shapes of the things around. What are you actually doing? What are you watching? What should you be paying attention to?

Shrinking tip 9 Feeling the feelings

The smirches want you to believe

that **everyone else** is free of bad feelings and feels totally fulfilled at work, at home and in their heads. They try to hide the fact that **ALL** experiences and relationships produce negative and positive feelings.

For your bag

Expansion techniques
A soothe box
A list of activities that help to absorb you when the smirch is winning

So the only way to keep free of negative feelings would be to have no contact with other humans or even pets. However, that probably won't make you feel happy either.

Think of any positive relationship or activity that you enjoy. This could be a pet, a neighbour, your closest friend or child, a good job, getting married or simply watching a film.

These all give many benefits, but with every relationship and meaningful activity there also comes:

Guilt	Anxiety	Fear	Distress	Sadness	Disappointment
'I have not seen my parents much.' 'I could be a better mum.'	'Will my child be ok?' 'Is this the right job for the future?'	'I will lose my job.' 'Will my partner leave?' 'I might fail.'	'My friend has cancer.' 'My child is being bullied.'	'I miss my son.' 'My cat died.' 'I forgot a work task.'	'I didn't get a pay rise.' 'My son is in trouble.'

All experiences and relationships produce the full range of normal human emotions, negative and positive. These are unavoidable, even when life is feeling relatively good. Smirches like to remind you of what your parents and teachers told you as children: boys don't cry, it's not that bad, don't make a fuss, put on a brave face.

Smirches want you to believe that you have the power to control bad feelings when they know humans can't do that.

When the bad feelings come they want you to believe you have negative feelings because you are weak, stupid or a failure in comparison to all the other people around you who certainly are not experiencing any bad feelings. Feelings are as changeable as the British weather. How much would we achieve if we chose only to go out or do anything meaningful if the weather was good? Smirches want us to be like that in response to our feelings.

Thought or feeling
Outcome

'I can't go out as I am feeling low.'
Avoid going out

'I will miss the party as it will make me anxious.'
Don't see friends

'I am too embarrassed to shop looking like this.'
Stop shopping

'I won't start a relationship until I feel better.'
Stay alone

'If I talk to them they will think I am stupid.'
Don't make new friends

'I will get the sack so I might as well resign.'
Leave job

The smirches are jumping with joy!

They are just delighted! They have made a mild bad feeling feel massive. Then you cancel your friend or take a day off work and growl at your children's noise and your partner's lack of help. They remind you that this bad phase can only get worse. They then slip in a tune that says you are a bad friend, colleague and mother and the guilty feelings are heaped on top of the growing pile making it an enormous bonfire-sized pile of terrible feelings.

Bad feelings are normal but humans don't like them. Often it is not the bad feelings that cause your distress but your struggle to be free of them, or what you do to try and get rid of them.

So what can you do?

Notice
You should be getting to understand the concept of noticing now. You are becoming more aware of your thoughts, your ups and downs. Now start to notice your feelings, the physical sensations in your body, your emotions.

Name that feeling
When you wake up, when you are doing different things, when you try to sleep, just notice what feelings come up, and try and label them. That's anxiety, that's fear, that's excitement, that's a low mood. See if you can notice when different emotions come. By noting in your journal you will start to see patterns. When does that smirch make me feel anxious? What was I doing? Try and see if you can notice what tunes or images the smirch has been playing or what situation you are in.

The smirch will not be happy if the 'thinking, feeling, doing' loop becomes clearer to you. He knows that will give you a massive surge of strength.

Smoggle
Tues 5th Oct
Smoggle is black and white with yellow spots and lots of spiky hair. He loves using his claw brush to make my skin feel really horrible sensations. He also loves to remind me of the time when I felt really scared and couldn't leave the house. I knew he was nearby today with his generating machine because I started to feel really scared and anxious.

The usual response when you notice a negative feeling is to feel uncomfortable.

Top three responses to a negative feeling:

- To feel anxious or stressed about having the feeling, to tense up and feel worse.

- To try and get rid of it by doing something. You probably have a favourite thing: exercising, going to bed, hurting yourself, shouting at others, drinking too much.

- To try and ignore it. The smirches make this option impossible as they will make sure the feeling grabs your attention with a good tune. 'Here it comes again', 'this is so horrid', 'you won't cope', are just a few of the favourites.

Some psychologists talk about a technique called **expansion** to manage those uncomfortable feelings: sadness, anger, distress or anxiety. This just means making room for your painful feelings without struggling.

The idea is to start by noticing the feeling and perhaps thinking about whether you are playing a tune that is causing it. Bad feelings are sometimes a bit like a smoke alarm; they alert us there is a problem. Often that problem is caused by what tunes and films are being played in our heads.

Expansion includes some things you already know about: belly breaths, noticing, connecting, naming the tunes and the feelings. It is really just learning not to tense up and panic in response to emotional discomfort. Have a good look at what you are actually feeling, as if you are a scientist investigating a new phenomenon which will make you rich if you can give a perfect description.

EXPANSION

- **When** you feel a bad feeling, take a few belly breaths and try and relax your body.
- **Pretend** you are seeing something new for the first time. Show interest.
- **Focus** on your body. Start at your head and work down.
- **Notice** where in your body the feeling is strongest.
- **Pretend** you are doing a study for a science project and discovering something new. What does it feel like? Where does it start and stop? Is it moving? Is it hot or cold?
- **Name** the emotion; say, 'here is fear'.
- **Continue** to observe.
- **Breathe** slowly and deeply.
- **Imagine** your breath flowing into your emotion: it's as if you are giving it space, not trying to push it out.
- **Notice** your body, notice your breath. You don't have to like it.
- **Try** and widen your focus so you can notice your body, what else you can see and hear.
- **Try** and do this until you feel that you can get on with what you need to do.

Practice Ideas

Try out the expansion technique when you experience mild discomfort eg if you stub your toe, feel too cold or too hot, or burn your finger. Take belly breaths, relax your body and try and notice what the pain is actually like, where it is most felt, whether it is continuous, throbbing etc.

A box in your bag

When you are really upset it can be hard to know what might help. This can sometimes make you do things that help in that moment but are not good for you in the long term. It can be useful to keep a soothe bag or box so that when you feel overwhelmingly distressed you can go to your bag or box and find something that will help. When you are feeling calm, collect together items that you know help when you feel upset. Include things that you can see, eat, feel and touch.

Do an activity that absorbs you

Think of a positive mental or physical activity to do despite your bad feelings, eg puzzle books, electronic games, make a picture or card, bake a cake, go for a walk etc.

Write a list of your ideas and keep it in your journal or soothe bag as sometimes it is hard to think when you are experiencing lots of bad feelings.

'In my soothe box I have a photo of my son and I laughing in the sea, I have a lovely card my husband wrote, some lavender oil, a bible verse, a small bar of chocolate and a list of things I can do that will help me feel better in the next hour like watching a DVD, looking out of the window or calling my friend.'

Kate

Allocate the smirch a strict time to visit (perhaps five minutes in the morning and evening, but not too near your bedtime). Give yourself this time to worry and think about your smirch, what he has made you think, feel and do. Write down your worries and what you are afraid of. Some fears might be real, some not, but whatever they are they will be much less scary on paper. 'I am afraid of dying, getting fat, losing my mind, being in a wheelchair, crying in public, failing, never working again.' Fears are much less useful to the smirch in black and white than when they are running as tunes in your head. Then practise some belly breaths and connect back to the present.

Practice Ideas

Anxiety is normal. We all feel it and will continue to feel it at times. Notice when you start to feel anxiety or panic. Don't struggle or fight with the feelings and thoughts. Just NOTICE – this is just a normal body response to unhelpful thoughts. It will pass.

Notice what makes you angry: times, places and people. Know the early signs: tense, breathing, hot, fists clenched. Plan and practise how to calm yourself, count to ten, walk away, say a calming phrase, focus on a photo of your child. Remember your values speech.

Shrinking tip 10 Clearing the smog: managing cognitive or thinking changes

Some smirches cause neurological damage that changes memory, problem solving, organising, multitasking and concentration and slows the speed of thinking.

Many smirches don't have such power but like to pretend they do. They play lots of tunes, cause lots of distractions and soon you can't concentrate, you start to forget things, feel chaotic and your thinking slows down, just because the smirch keeps pulling you onto autopilot.

Then they play some lyrics such as 'perhaps you are insane, you are beginning to get senile, you are too old'. These tunes make you feel scared and then you struggle with your fears and bad feelings and you forget even more. The smirches are happy when you feel totally paralysed and overwhelmed by the demands placed on you.

It doesn't matter how your smirch inflicts changes to thinking as the strategies that help are much the same.

'Fail to plan, plan to fail'

is a well-known phrase that smirches don't like as it tells of a very useful lifeline. Smirches thrive on chaos and hate structure, routine and planning because they know this helps everyone. Developing the habit of planning each day will help in so many ways. It is often helpful to keep planning sheets in a file together with an ongoing 'to do' list. All you really need is a piece of paper or a section in your journal where you can write the times and tasks you intend to do.

For your bag

Planning sheets and 'To do' list

Planning Sheet

Activity	Time start	Time finish	Rest/ Activity	Don't forget
Getting up routine	7.30	8.00	A	
Breakfast and clearing up	8.00	8.30	A	
Do kids' lunches	8.30	8.45	A	
Do planning for day	9.00	9.15	A	Sally over for coffee
Have coffee with a friend	9.30	11.30	R	
Wash up	11.30	11.45	A	
Have lunch	12.00	1.00	R	
Do prep for dinner	1.15	2.15	A	
Have a cup of tea & rest	2.30	3.30	R	Oscar dentist 4pm
Spend time with kids	3.30	4.30	R	
Cook tea	4.45	5.30	A	
Dinner with family & clear up	5.30	6.30	A	
Put kids to bed	7.00	7.30	A	Great British Bake off! :)8pm
Watch TV	7.30	8.30	R	
Hobby time	8.30	9.30	R	
Bedtime routine	9.30	9.45	A	
Read	9.45	10.15	R	
Sleep	10.15	7.30	R	

Practice Ideas

Put planning sheets and to do lists into an image search engine and there are lots of different ideas. Some larger stationers now sell weekly desk pads and planners.

Good habits are as hard to forget as bad ones, so use this to your advantage. Each day, preferably in the morning, set aside half an hour to plan.

Handy Tips for Planning

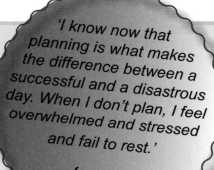

- Have a space in your home where you always plan—a notice board would help.

- When you plan, have with you your calendar, diary, phone and 'to do' list.

- Sit down with a plan of the day and allocate tasks to specific times.

- Remind yourself of any appointments you must remember and allocate them to the time. Don't forget to mark in sufficient time for travelling without a rush and also note anything you need to take with you to the appointment.

- Include a balance of rest and activity.

- Don't allow contact with too many drains **but see plenty of fountains.**

- Plan regular meals and drinks of water: it may help to decide what you need to cook and plan time for meal preparation and clearing up.

- Make sure each day that you have included activities that give you a sense of achievement, bring contact with others and give you pleasure.

- Cast an eye to your calendar for the next week and month. Do you need more rest days to stock up on resources, so the smirch doesn't stop you enjoying a significant event or challenge?

Look at your plan and decide if it is reasonable. Would this be a fair plan if you were asking a friend to achieve it?

Follow your plan as closely as you can and tick off each thing as you achieve it. Imagine you are being watched by a manager who insists you stick to your plan.

Planning will help focus your attention. It will free up your mind from all the tasks and make you less likely to forget. If you are using your journal, you will soon start to see what is proving too much or too little.

Prepare	Set time aside each day and be realistic.
List	Write down the plan and prioritise.
Act	Do it regardless of what your smirch makes you think or feel.
Notice	Notice how each activity impacts you.

At the end of each day try and take a few minutes to reflect. Ask yourself what went well, what didn't and what you would do differently if you could go back in time. Make a note of useful answers in your journal.

Smoggle
Tues 5th Oct
Smoggle is black and white with yellow spots and lots of spiky hair. He loves using his claw brush to make my skin feel really horrible sensations. He also loves to remind me of time when I felt really

Practice Ideas

- Prioritize your to do list; A – urgent, must be done, B – be good if done today, C – not really important can wait.

- In your reflection time make sure you add any unfinished tasks to the next day's list.

- Keep information and important items (keys, wallet, address book etc) in the same place.

- Repeat information to yourself.

- Use memory aids wherever possible, such as a diary or calendar.

- Do one thing at a time and remove distractions wherever possible, eg noise, television people.

- Use prompts to start and continue activities, eg alarm clocks, mobile phones.

- Don't rush or overload yourself. Break down big tasks into small steps.

Shrinking tip 11 Problem solving

The smirches like you to feel overwhelmed with all your problems muddled together. They make sure they keep it all going round in your head unsolved so you feel anxious and fearful, as everything feels unmanageable.

Learn to make use of pen and paper frequently. When your head feels fit to burst, the smirch feels strong and you feel like running away or going to bed. List the things that are bothering you. Include the small things and the bigger things.

Then work through these six Ps:

For your bag

A problem-solving template

Problem-solving Template Example

The problem I have too much to do.

Who is involved in this problem? I am involved but also others who make demands on me.
What makes this a problem? It makes me feel stressed.
When and how often does the problem occur? All the time.
Where does it occur? At home.
What makes it worse and better? Rest, planning and asking others to help. Saying no.
Possible solutions: Do less, ask for help. Say no.

Solutions: Write down everything I have to do.
Ask what can I cancel or withdraw from.
What can I ask others to do?
Get back into planning every day.

My goals: I will write a chore list for the children.
I will plan every morning when the kids go to school.
I will go for a swim on a Tuesday at 11.
When someone asks me to do something, I will learn to say 'can I let you know?' so I have time to consider it properly.

1 Problem statement

Write the problem in clear words so anyone could understand what you mean.
Eg 'I am in pain.'
'My son might get hurt at school.'
'I might fail my exam.'
'I will lose my job.'
'I have too much to do.'

2 Problem details

Ask yourself the following questions:
Who is involved in this problem? What makes this a problem? When and how often does the problem occur?
Where does it occur?
What makes it worse and better?

3 Possible solutions

Brainstorm all the possible solutions.
Some solutions will be easy and quick, others may take months to resolve.

4 Pros and cons of each solution

Look at each possible solution and think about what the positive and negatives would be of using that solution. Ask others what they think too.

5 Pick the best solution or solutions

6 Plan action step by step

Make sure your action plan is so clear that someone else could follow your steps. Can you change your solution to a SMART goal to add to your journal?

Problem-solving Template Example

The Problem I have too much to do.

Who is involved in this problem? I am involved but also others who make demands on me.

What makes this a problem? It makes me feel stressed.

When and how often does the problem occur? All the time.

Where does it occur? At home.

What makes it worse and better? Rest, planning and asking others to help. Saying no.

Possible solutions: Do less, ask for help, say no.

Solutions Write down everything I have to do.

Ask what can I cancel or withdraw from.
What can I ask others to do?
Get back into planning every day.

My goals I will write a chore list for the children.

I will plan every morning when the kids go to school.
I will go for a swim on a Tuesday at 11:00.
When someone asks me to do something, I will say 'Can
I let you know?' so I have time to consider it properly.

Practice Ideas

Put into an image search engine: 'problem-solving sheet' and you will see lots of ideas you could copy for your problem-solving template.

The smirch will be keen to play you some old tunes: 'you will fail', 'remember last time', 'give up', 'what's the point of writing it down', 'ignore it'. The smirch knows you will feel so much better if you can disentangle and talk about the problems rather than keep them in your head

Chapter 6: Body Stuff...

In this section we are looking at a number of physical health issues:

- **Food and drink**
- **Pain**
- **Fatigue**
- **Exercise**
- **Rest**

Your journal will be key to defeating your smirch in these areas.

Each issue is different but some key principles apply to all.
You can remember these principles as the 3 As

1 Assess
This is where you find a way to keep accurate records about what is happening in each area. Put space in your diary to record food, mood, pain, physical activity, rest etc

2 Analyse
Use the journal to work out how each health issue corresponds to your good and bad days and the size of your smirch. Look for patterns, eg *'When I get the balance right between rest and activity, my smirch is smaller.' 'When I stay hydrated, I feel brighter.' 'When I am in pain, I am more likely to stay in bed.'*

3 Act
Choose a SMART goal to help you do fewer of the unhelpful things and more of the things that take you towards your chosen values.

Shrinking tip 12 Exhausting your smirch

For your bag
A pedometer

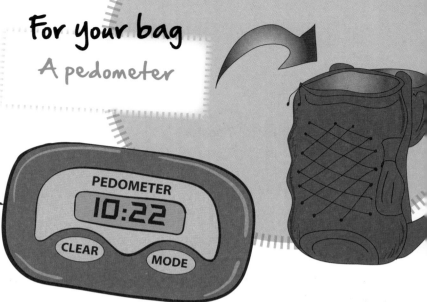

Smirches are very lazy

They like to irritate humans with little effort. They know that humans are easy targets when they are alone, doing nothing and caught up in their heads. Smirches find sweat very unpleasant and so if you are active they will stay away. They also prefer not to move very much, so if you are moving you already have the upper hand.

RESEARCH ALERT

CONFIDENTIAL TOP SECRET CONFIDENTIAL

Exercise stimulates the brain chemicals that make you feel better.

Twenty minutes of exercise three times a week (even walking) is better for mild to moderate depression than medication.

Smirches know that physical activity has lots of amazing side effects.
Exercise improves joints and bones and backs, makes bladders and bowels function better, lowers cholesterol and blood pressure and even helps thinking and memory. No wonder smirches hate people exercising. They will try all their top tunes to try and keep you still. '*You are too disabled/fat/anxious to move*', '*you will feel terrible*', '*it will make your fatigue worse*', '*people will stare at you*'.

Beware then. They will fight this battle hard as they know that even a little more moving can make you feel so much better in your body and mind.

If you notice and connect as you move

this will be even more beneficial to your mind and body and thus moving more will have a double shrinking value.

Remember the 3 As principles

Assess

How much are you moving?
Keep a record of how much activity you do in a day. Maybe a pedometer will help to count your steps if you can walk.

Analyse

What impact are your activity levels having on your life?
Maybe you're exercising too much! Perhaps you are not moving enough or overdoing it some days and staying in bed on others.

Act

Set a SMART goal to take you closer to where you want to be.
For example: 'I am going to stop using exercise to suppress bad feelings.'
'I am going to walk for 20 minutes on Mondays, Tuesdays and Fridays.'

RESEARCH ALERT

For every hour of TV watched you walk 144 fewer steps. Get up in the adverts, even if just to make a hot drink.

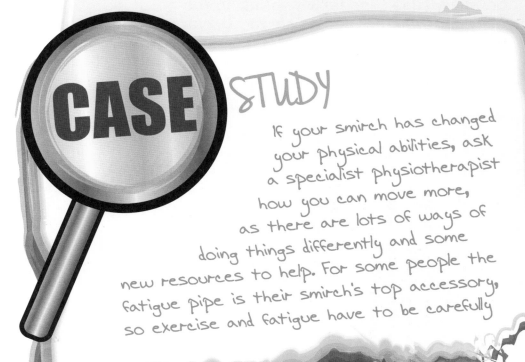

CASE STUDY

If your smirch has changed your physical abilities, ask a specialist physiotherapist how you can move more, as there are lots of ways of doing things differently and some new resources to help. For some people the fatigue pipe is their smirch's top accessory, so exercise and fatigue have to be carefully

Shrinking tip 13 Dining with your smirch

Smirches rejoice every time a new diet book comes out.

They know that adds to the confusion and people struggle for a few weeks trying the new ideas: more carbs, less protein, no fruit, milkshakes, cabbage, fewer carbs, more protein, GI, points, red and green, five to two, etc. Smirches know generally the old habits soon return as this all becomes too confusing and unmanageable in real life.

Smirches like the fact that people go back quickly to their old ways of eating too much sugar and fat and drinking too much alcohol and fizz. They don't really care whether people are fat, thin or in-between, but they do care a lot about mood. They know that a few days or weeks of consistent high sugar eating and drinking too much will inevitably lead to bad feelings—another of their favourite things.

FAT!

The smirches know

... that when the bingeing comes after a period of 'being good' the tunes are more effective. *'You failed again', 'look at the state of you', 'your partner will leave', 'people think you are stupid'.* They know if a few extra glasses of wine are involved, thinking gets less rational and the actions become less conscious and more autopilot.

Ignore all the diet books. The rules are simple and there are some helpful websites about eating well on the reference list.

For your bag

A food and mood section in your journal

RESEARCH ALERT

CONFIDENTIAL TOP SECRET CONFIDENTIAL

- Keep treat food out of sight. If you can't see it you are less likely to eat it.

- People drink less if they use a tall thin glass rather than a short fat one.

- Food changes our mood, drink changes what we think!

Practice Ideas

- Feel your emotions, don't feed them.

- Throw away the weighing scales. They are the smirches' best weapon to bring on bad feeling.

In a nutshell what your grandma said was right

'Breakfast is the most important meal of the day, skip at your peril.'

'Keep the treats small and less frequent.'

'Eat more fruit and vegetables and less processed food and the smirches will shake with fear.'

'Have three smaller meals and three small snacks to keep your blood sugar levels stable across the day.'

'High sugar foods change blood sugar levels which change mood and energy levels.'

Smaller changes introduced one at a time are easier to manage and keep up. If you make more than one change at a time you won't be able to tell what is having an effect.

Smirches know it is small changes that work, small changes that can be lifelong, not days long. They like humans to eat too much or too little, and to eat on autopilot. The smirches thrive when humans don't notice what they are eating and drinking.

'After years of diets I have found success. I am making small changes I can achieve. I don't have toast on a Tuesday, I have given up butter on bread on weekends.'

RESEARCH ALERT

CONFIDENTIAL
TOP SECRET
CONFIDENTIAL

Drinking too much alcohol leads to serious physical and mental illnesses.

Practice Ideas

A healthy diet includes a wide variety of foods. Is there any one food or type of food that you eat nearly every day or in particularly large amounts?

If you suddenly stop drinking coffee or chocolate, you may get withdrawal symptoms, such as headaches or cravings. Symptoms can be reduced if you cut down gradually.

Alcohol is the smirches' best friend.

Alcohol changes brain function and makes you care less about what you say and do. Alcohol can also magnify your bad feelings. This is one of the reasons that many people become angry or aggressive when drinking. If your feelings are of anxiety, anger or unhappiness, alcohol can make them feel worse, which is why most smirches play the tune 'go on have a drink, it will help you cope, make you feel better, make you more sociable'.

Smirches know that drinking only numbs feelings for a short time. People who suffer from anxiety and depression have even worse symptoms when the effects of alcohol wear off.

So back to the 3 As

Assess
Notice that hand-to-mouth movement that is often done on autopilot. Record everything you eat and drink (or, if easier, all you buy) in your journal and just notice.

Analyse
Become more aware of the patterns. Do you eat more processed foods at certain times of the day or the month? Do you use food to blot out bad feelings? Do you eat too little or too infrequently? How does what you consume impact your feelings, sleep, fatigue, thinking and mood that day and the day after?

Act
Choose a smart goal relating to food and drink.
For example: *'I will drink two more glasses of water during my day'*, *'I will have one fewer bar of chocolate a week'*, *'I will not drink alcohol on three week days'*, *'when I am anxious I will try and do something else to manage my feelings before I have food.'*

RESEARCH ALERT

- The most vital substance for a healthy mind and body is water. The recommended six to eight glasses per day can quickly change how we feel, mentally as well as physically. Eg

Eg

- Having a minimum of five portions daily of fresh fruit and vegetables will provide the nutrients needed to nourish mind and body.

- Using smaller plates and spoons makes you eat less without noticing.

- A mirror in the kitchen makes you eat less.

- Low levels of the mineral zinc can make eating disorders more likely and low levels of omega-3 oils have been linked with depression.

- Too much caffeine (which is a different amount for each of us) can cause symptoms of anxiety and cause sleep difficulties.

Shrinking tip 14 Pain

Some smirches are masters of physical pain as well as psychological pain.

They use the same principles for both:

- Wait for it to happen.
- Quickly bring your focus onto it.
- Make the pain worse by lots of timely tunes: *'Here it comes, you won't cope, it's a bad sign, you are getting worse'.*

The physical and mental pain then becomes much worse and you stop doing what you want to do or do the things you don't want to do—such as using alcohol to suppress feelings, shouting at your family or just going to bed.

For your bag...

A pain scale in your journal

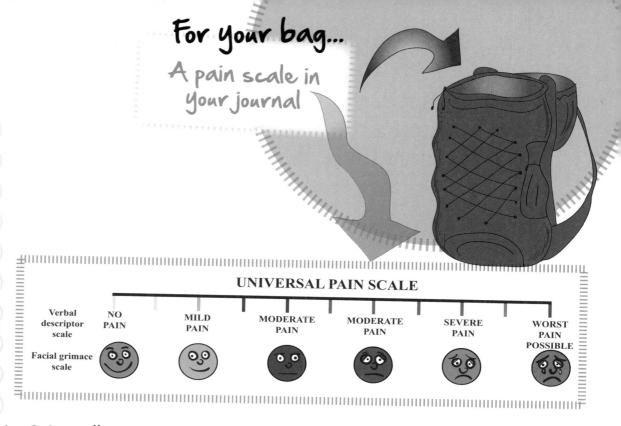

This is getting repetitive but hopefully you will soon have the 3 As well established in your mind:

ASSESS

The first step is noticing. Keep a good record of your pain in your diary. Try and record where the pain is, the intensity, the type of pain and how long it lasts. Ideally record your pain experience on three occasions per day at the same times. This means you are more likely to see patterns. Jot down what is happening and a score of 1–10, or use a pain scale.

ANALYSE

Notice when it is most likely, what factors make it worse or better: the weather, fatigue, over-activity, sleeping, 'draining people'. Think about how much is actual pain and how much is due to the struggles with the smirches' tunes and pictures. Notice what the tunes and pictures are.

ACT

Think about how you might want to change your activities to improve your pain. Talk to others who experience pain, about what helps them. Then set one or two SMART goals.
For example, *'I am going to practise some of my expansion techniques and belly breaths at least once a day so that I can try them when I am in pain'.*
'I am going to ask for a referral to see a pain specialist'.

Use your accurate recordings to gang up on your smirch with any specialists that you see about your pain. They might be able to give you medication or other skills to have in your resource bag.

Type 'pain scale' into a search engine for ideas

Shrinking tip 15 Managing the Fatigue

Some smirches use their fatigue pipe more than anything else

You might be someone who is constantly depleted of energy because you live with a very specialist smirch.

Other smirches don't use their fatigue pipes much because they know that poor diets, not moving much, too much alcohol, overworking and a head that is consumed with tunes is enough to produce fatigue and exhaustion.

Smirches know that humans have a tendency to want to succeed, rush and achieve perfection. They know these tendencies make it hard to manage fatigue.

The smirch has whole albums of tunes dedicated to keeping humans feeling shattered. The favourites are:

'What will people think if you don't have a spotless house?' *'You must take a homemade pudding.'* *'What if the neighbours knew when you last changed the bedding? Your friends would be disgusted!'* *'Just ten more minutes cleaning.'*

For your bag

Some fact sheets on fatigue management from the websites in the resource section.

A word the smirches hate is 'pacing'
They know this is the answer to improve fatigue in most people.

Pacing means not doing too much or pushing yourself until you collapse, but also not doing too little. A little exercise each day improves energy levels. Do tasks more slowly and take regular breaks and the smirch will quake.

'I have always worried the kids will become carers but I realise they are quite lazy. They are now changing their bedding and tidying their rooms once a week. This gives me extra time and energy to do something nice with them.'

Kate

The smirches will tell you: *'Go it alone.'* *'Don't ask the kids to help.'* *'That makes you a bad mother.'* If you ask a neighbour to buy some milk the smirches will tell you: *'The whole road will be chatting about Mrs Lazy!'* Delegation is something you have to learn to defeat these smirches. Most people want to help if you let them, and you can then keep your energy for the really important things.

Many smirches aim also to disturb sleep.

They know this makes your mind and body cope less well with life. Everyone needs different amounts of sleep to cope, so experiment with bed and wake-up times. When you have worked out from your journal what works best, try as hard as possible to go to bed and get up at the same time. Your body likes this, the smirch will not.

Smirches often play their tunes the loudest at night. Write down any issues that are on your mind before you go to bed, notice what tunes are playing, do some belly breaths and use your expansion techniques.

RESEARCH ALERT

Children who are encouraged to help with the household tasks grow up feeling more confident.

Managing mood, diet, sleep and learning to relax can boost energy levels.

RESEARCH ALERT

- Wind down for half an hour before bed.
- If you are not asleep in 20 minutes, get up.
- Change your bedroom to ensure it is dark, quiet and comfortable.
- Avoid caffeine, smoking and alcohol near to bedtime.

The 3 As

Assess
Keep a record of what you are doing, when and for how long. Note bed and wake times.

Analyse
Watch for patterns. When are you most fatigued? Can you see anything in your mood, lifestyle or activity levels that makes you sleep less well or changes fatigue levels?

Act
Think about what needs changing. Do you need to do some activities for a shorter time? Can you change the time of a meeting to be at your best time of the day? Can some draining activities be dropped or given to someone else? Are you putting regular rest breaks into your daily plan and sticking to them?

You may want to look at some of the references at the back of this book on how to manage fatigue before you decide on some SMART goals.

Eg
- 'I will only iron essentials.'
- 'I am going to rest for half an hour at 11:00 every day and sit down for the evening by 20.00.'
- 'I am going to give up the school committee.'

'I feel guilty that I can't do more and sometimes slip into doing too much as the smirch plays good tunes such as: "You are so lazy, your house is filthy". I am getting better at not listening as I now know that when I do too much I feel much worse for the next three days.'

Kate

'On Saturdays I felt I had to clean the car, do all my paper work and the shopping. I have started taking the car to a car wash once a month, I now shop online and I put aside an hour a week to do essential admin; the rest can wait. Now I have more time to watch TV and relax so I can cope better in the week.'

Colin

Practice Ideas

- Break down larger jobs like cleaning the house into smaller ones. Hoover one room, not the whole house.

- If you know your specialist smirch is known to be good at causing fatigue, name it something different like FATTIGAR. This means people don't understand the term and you can explain that it is a physical symptom and part of your condition, like MS, chronic fatigue, lupus or stroke. It is NOT just tiredness like other people experience.

Shrinking tip 16 Have at least one day of rest

Until a few decades ago most western societies were forced into a day of rest. Shops closed and businesses stopped on a Sunday, if not all weekend. Desk tops stayed on desks. Increasingly this is not the case and humans are being made to feel they should be working 24/7. The problem with this is that our minds and bodies have not been created to live like this and smirches know that.

For your bag

A personal and family rest plan. A box for gadgets to sleep

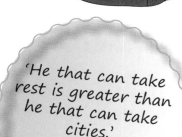

Shhh! gadgets resting

'He that can take rest is greater than he that can take cities.'

Benjamin Franklin

George Nachman described his perceptions of a seven-day week in the *Chicago Tribune*.

THE CHICAGO TRIBUNE

No 301/076   THE WORLD'S MOST READ NEWSPAPER

'I looked out of the window and discovered Sunday had disappeared. Nobody had swiped it exactly, [I guess he doesn't know about the smirches] but something had gone. I realised that Sunday had turned into Tuesday. Out on the street, people were no longer strolling about. They had direction, a mid-week glint in their eyes that meant business. They were walking briskly in and out of shops instead of browsing quietly past the windows. The scene was as busy as your average workday. Now all seven days are workdays!'

RESEARCH ALERT

CONFIDENTIAL TOP SECRET CONFIDENTIAL

Seventy five per cent of people have a smart phone or tablet but constant use is causing health and relationship problems. Excessive use of electronic gadgets can also lead to a drooping jawline, wrinkles, neck and skin problems.

Smirches just love gadgets.

They love their own gadgets but also the full range of human gadgets that have emerged. These gadgets may be described as 'smart' gadgets, but they pull us into our heads more often than the smirches. How many times have you been playing with the kids, shopping or reading when bleep goes the device and straight away the smirch has you in its grasp?

Smirches agree there is nothing smarter that something that can instantly pull you away from a chat with a real person or a relaxing television drama. Electronic devices such as phones and tablets so easily put thoughts into your head to panic you about a meeting, a deal that has gone wrong or an overdraft alert from the bank.

Smirches love these electronic gadgets as they know they often hinder intimate relationships and can create physical and mental health problems.

Smirches are getting slightly anxious

... as top scientists are reportedly working on smart watches and smart glasses. So smirches are wondering whether they will be made redundant. The smirches are worrying that people will be so stressed and caught up in their heads that they may not even have time to be disturbed by them.

We have lost an agreed weekly day of rest, but increasingly for many an hour of rest is becoming rare. Smirches have a well-devised set of tunes to make resting unlikely: *'Rest is for the weak'*, *'You will get the sack'*, *'You will miss an important email'*. Physical muscles need rest days to recover and get even stronger.
Our minds equally need rest. More work is NOT better work.

Smirches love to see humans on the hamster wheel so they have no rest time to strengthen their relationships, take a step back or evaluate their lives. They love to see you with a lifestyle that focuses on your possessions not your values. They know that with every new car, designer item and bigger kitchen, relationships weaken and resources are drained. This in turn makes people more vulnerable to their games.

They know that concentrated rest will build up reserves for when the unexpected emergencies of life strike.

RESEARCH ALERT

CONFIDENTIAL TOP SECRET

Many people check their phones up to 150 times a day. There is now even a name for excessive phone use, 'Infomania'!

So to conclude

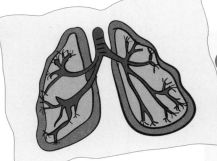

1 Assess

Look at your journal and see when you are actually taking proper rest.

2 Analyse

Look for patterns as to how over-working impacts how you think, feel and behave.

3 Act

Aim to have at least one day of rest.
If you live within a family, plan together. Choose creative activities that are refreshing and encourage relationships. Decide that at certain times and days all gadgets will also be put to rest and out of reach of hand or mind.

Practice Ideas

- If you have a spare five minutes, try to resist reaching for an electronic device. Practise belly breaths and connecting to the world around you.

- Constant phone-checking creates feelings of stress and anxiety. See if you can practise having breaks from your phones and tablets. Put it in another room for two or three hours every day. Leave it at home when you go out for an evening. Breaking the phone-checking habit will be hard, but see how much less stressed you feel when you get used to these phone-breaks.

Set SMART goals

to allow you and your gadgets to rest.
For example, 'every Sunday afternoon we will go out as a family for a walk or drive.'
'After 19:30 on Mondays to Thursdays the gadgets will go in another room.'
'I will sit down with my wife every Friday to plan some rest time together.'

Shhh! gadgets resting

Chapter 7: The Final Touches

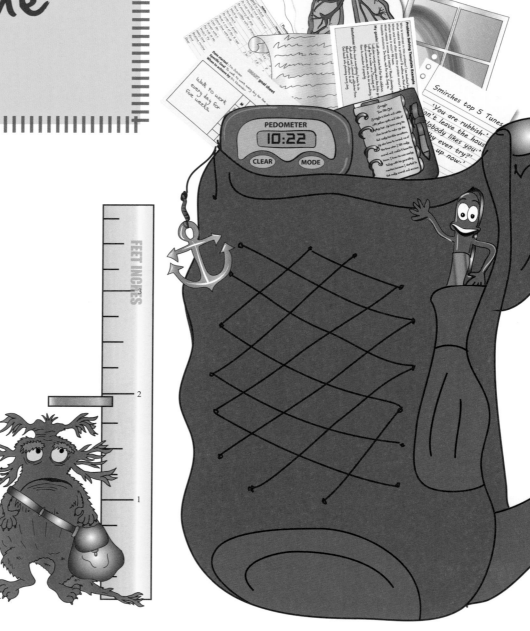

Shrinking tip 17 Ganging up on your smirch

We already know smirches love to keep people isolated and alone with no tunes but their own. They love it when you don't tell people how you feel, return to bed and turn down an invite. They know that when it is just you in the shrinking game they have more chance of staying big.

So get a gang

In your gang or team you need people who can give you accurate information, social support, emotional support and practical help. One person can't do it all, so think about who are the people in your life who can supply you with what you need.

Talk to the people who care about you

If you don't, they feel shut out and helpless and you feel disappointed at their lack of help or inappropriate offers of support. Recognise when the smirch is winning and tell others. Ask them to help.

Be specific in how you feel and what you need:

'When I have a relapse I need more hugs.'
'Please don't leave your school bag where I will trip.'
'When I am in pain, support me to move more.'
'If I am feeling low, hand me my soothe box, encourage me to watch TV or go for a walk.'

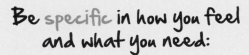

For your bag

A list of people to be in your shrinking gang

My smirch gang

My neighbour Pat
My Mum
My partner
My doctor
My pain specialist
My best friend Sue

CONFIDENTIAL
TOP SECRET

RESEARCH ALERT

To strengthen your relationship, spend ten minutes writing down your deepest feelings about that person.

Write down one of your partner's most endearing qualities and why it means a lot to you.

Get a friendly dog; dog owners are less stressed, happier and healthier than others! Watching even a ten-minute video of some cute animals can have the same calming effect.

Never turn down an offer of help

Think of ideas before the situation arises. When someone says 'Can I help?', say thank you with a big smile and give a very specific request.

A meal for the freezer would be lovely!
An hour of ironing would help so much.
An evening's babysitting would be amazing!
'Id love some help with this problem.
A coffee and a chat would really help.

RESEARCH ALERT

CONFIDENTIAL
TOP SECRET
CONFIDENTIAL

People like you more if you ask for help!

People who go to church regularly and participate in the associated social activities seem to have more ability to cope with life's challenges.

Practice Ideas

- If people ask for present ideas at Christmas and birthdays, have ready some practical help ideas written on cards (eg one hour of ironing, one evening of babysitting, one room hoovered) and say, 'I have everything I need but any of these things would help enormously to shrink my smirch!'

- Write a blog about your smirch and his favourite tunes and tricks and what you are doing to shrink your smirch.

Some health conditions have specialist nurses and professionals available for advice and support. Make sure you use these people well. Prepare before an appointment by writing down issues or questions and take a dictaphone to record answers. Your detailed journal will give you much clearer information to share on diet, pain, mood and the goals for which you need support.

74

If you have a new symptom for more than a few weeks

make sure you speak to your GP and get them to join your shrinking gang. Smirches love you to give them the credit for other difficulties, but this time it might be an unrelated condition.

If your smirch represents a named condition, get accurate information from only one or two sources. The internet is a great resource but some forums and sites mislead people. It is important that any information you get about how a typical smirch like yours works and gets created is based on scientific research and NOT the opinion of a few individuals. Your GP would be a good person to ask about sources of good information for your specific smirch. There are some reputable sites for many smirch conditions at the back of this workbook.

'The smirch threw up an interesting bond between my teenage daughter and me. We had never really talked in depth about the challenges my smirch throws up. Drawing and talking about the smirch together gave us both the opportunity for discussion and understanding.'

Ian

It can be great to talk to others who also have to live with a smirch but some forums are so negative or untruthful that they can give the smirch new ideas for bad tunes to play. So be careful that you notice the impact these forums have on how you think and feel and make sure they are fountains.

RESEARCH ALERT

CONFIDENTIAL TOP SECRET CONFIDENTIAL

Spend at least one hour a week talking to someone you trust about how things really are.

Get someone to just listen but not speak for five minutes a day.

Shrinking tip 18
Looking for the gold and being grateful

The understanding that

suffering and distress can lead to better personal qualities is thousands of years old. Smirches know that bad feelings, ill health and suffering can strangely be quite good for people's minds and relationships.

> **The questions the smirches most dread you asking are:**
> *'Could this bring anything positive?' 'How might this experience help me get closer to the person I want to be?' 'What practical skills might I learn or improve?'*

Of course if you start thinking about these questions the smirch will not be happy and he will find some appropriate lyrics to play: *'Don't be so stupid!' 'How can this be good?' 'This can only get worse.' 'Why me?' 'Nothing good will ever happen to me.' 'People are looking at me.'*

For your bag
A section in your journal for gratitude

Gratitude

Monday 22nd June

My husband told me how nice I looked today.
The pain wasn't as bad this week as I have been practising belly breaths.
My appointment with the specialist went well.
My neighbour came for coffee and brought me some flowers.

Shrinking Sm...
journa...

RESEARCH ALERT
CONFIDENTIAL — TOP SECRET — CONFIDENTIAL

Positive psychological changes in response to challenging life circumstances include a greater appreciation of life, changed priorities, feeling mentally stronger, having new opportunities, better relationships and new friends.

RESEARCH ALERT
CONFIDENTIAL — TOP SECRET — CONFIDENTIAL

Reports of personal growth stories in response to physical and psychological challenges far outnumber reports of psychiatric symptoms.

Can you start noticing that a lot of the bad feelings are due to listening to the smirchs' tunes

and not what is actually happening to you? Can you start connecting with the world? If you have been practising noticing and connecting perhaps you have already started to appreciate the small things you had previously ignored: the smell of cut grass, the sound of your children giggling, the feel of a warm bath or a kind touch.

Someone who had recovered after a life-threatening illness described themselves as 'being part of the blue sky club'. Often those who have life-challenging difficulties are the people who know what is really important: not possessions and achievements but who we are and our closeness to others. Can you seek the treasure and plan the pleasure? Look for things that are good and practise being thankful for them.

GOLD

Smirches want you to feel ungrateful; they want you to think a lot about the times you have been unfairly treated, the difficulties you have to deal with and the people who let you down.

They like to see you unhappy and trapped and they know a strange secret that has been proven to be true. Being grateful is helpful for the body, mind and relationships.

Someone once said

'Happiness is like the favourite perfume you get used to'. It is still as good as when you first smelt it but you have become accustomed to it and it no longer grabs your conscious attention – you don't notice.'

Practice Ideas

– Seek opportunities you know you will enjoy, rather than feeling disappointed as nothing nice has happened today. Plan one pleasurable thing each day.

RESEARCH ALERT

CONFIDENTIAL TOP SECRET CONFIDENTIAL

Being grateful is helpful for the body, mind and relationships.

Whatever challenges the smirch can throw, everyone has things that give at least momentary pleasure.

Practice Ideas

- Think about your amazing body even if you are ill or have lost many abilities. Think about your complex brain which is allowing you to read and think, feel and talk. Remember what your body has achieved: breathing, childbirth, fighting infection and mending bones.

'I hate being a carer but I tried really hard to start a gratitude diary. It was hard at first to find even one thing I felt grateful for. Today I wrote five things for the first time: the sun was shining, I got praise from a customer, my wife said "thank you", I feel a bit stronger and I found fifty pence!'

Colin

RESEARCH ALERT

CONFIDENTIAL
TOP SECRET
CONFIDENTIAL

- Think of a great day. Spend a few minutes thinking about all the details: the sights, sounds and what you can hear and feel. Close your eyes, take some belly breaths and enjoy the memory.

- Think about someone special and write a short letter or card to express your thanks.

RESEARCH ALERT

CONFIDENTIAL
TOP SECRET
CONFIDENTIAL

Things to write in your journal each day:

-Five things for which you are grateful.
-Think about someone you love and write for 20 minutes on what they mean to you and why.
-Think back over the past week and list three things for which you have been grateful.
-Think over last week and note all the things that went well, however small.

Shrinking tip 19 Kill your smirch with kindness

We are instructed to 'Love our neighbours as ourselves'.

If you were consistently to treat others like you treat yourself, would that be good for the other person?

For your bag

A list of ways YOU can be kind to YOU

Are you kind to yourself?
Would you allow your friend or child to be bullied by the smirchs' negative lyrics?

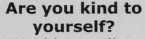

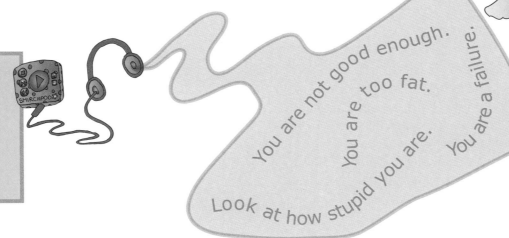

You are not good enough.

You are too fat.

Look at how stupid you are.

You are a failure.

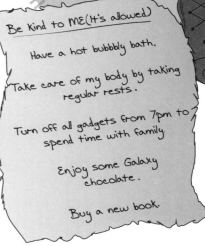

Be kind to ME (It's allowed)

Have a hot bubbbbly bath.

Take care of my body by taking regular rests.

Turn off all gadgets from 7pm to spend time with family.

Enjoy some Galaxy chocolate.

Buy a new book.

Would you

Treat your best friend or a child with kindness by feeding them too much food, food that makes them feel terrible, mentally and physically?	**Shut** your friend away and not let them meet with others or share their true feelings or even notice they are suffering?	**Make** your friend work 24/7 without regular breaks and treat them harshly when they failed because of fatigue or depression?	**Make** your friend keep their gadgets switched on all day so they never had any peace of mind?	**Hand** your friend a bottle of vodka when they feel sad or suggest they work some more?

This is NOT the picture of a good friend, except maybe a smirch's best friend!

Most humans are quite good at being kind to others

but treating yourself with kindness is much harder. You need to be kind to yourself as much as possible but especially when you are hurting or finding life a challenge.

You are the only person who truly understands what you have been through and what you feel. Think about someone you love. If they were experiencing suffering as you are, what would you do to support, care and comfort them? Write a list. This might include: practical help, a kind word, really listening to their feelings or a hug. This is the kind of approach you need to develop towards yourself.

Your smirch of course, is much happier when you are listening to his negative tunes, starving yourself of comfort or companionship and doing things that will make you feel worse. The first step is to actually notice when you are suffering. Can you then start to notice your reaction to yourself when you are in pain and connect with what you are feeling rather than pushing it away? Build in activities every day that will give you pleasure or make you feel loved and supported, rather than bullied and abandoned. When you hurt, your smirch wants to tell you that you are alone and everyone else is happy. Remind yourself this is a lie, all humans suffer and experience negative thoughts and bad feelings. Tell the smirch that they are only words and sensations and that you can accept them without fighting.

Practice Ideas

- Treat yourself as a best friend when you are hurting or have failed.

- Write a list of things that would make you feel well-treated by yourself: Bath with special bubble bath, read a good novel, watch a funny film, go for a swim, go for a walk or eat something delicious.

- Eat chocolate slowly, tasting every mouthful.

- Each day as you plan, decide three things you will do or say to treat yourself as a friend.

Smirches want to stop you
helping others as they know it makes humans feel happier and more content. So look for someone you can help out even in small ways, eg listening to a problem. The smirch will shudder at the thought of people joining your shrinking adventure.

RESEARCH ALERT

CONFIDENTIAL TOP SECRET CONFIDENTIAL

Smile at a smirch!
If you behave as if you are happy, sit up straight and smile for 15 to 30 seconds, the brain thinks you are happy and you feel happier. Put up stickers of smiley faces at home and at work to remind you to smile.

Shrinking tip 20 You are not your smirch!

If you have a psychological or physical health label, it is easy for your smirch to make you think that is all you are. Specialists sometimes even help with this by seeing you as a condition rather than an individual with a set of challenges. Smirches like it when you can only see your symptoms or diagnosis: I am an MS patient, a depressive, an anorexic or neurotic.

Remind the smirch who you are! Think about the strengths you have that are unchanged.

Think about positive activities you have given up because of a lack of time or difficulties. Is it worth trying to start again? Sometimes you might have to ask for help to achieve it in a different way or at another time.

You are a human being not a human doing. You may have had to give up lots of activities because of your challenges, but that doesn't change who you are, your values.

Practice Ideas

– Ask a supportive friend or family member to write a list of what they like about you and wave it at the smirch when his tunes start playing.

For your bag

A picture of yourself looking very happy and a list of all your achievements and future plans

'I realised that I had stopped being me. I used to love going out but my fatigue stops me. I think I am a rubbish mum as I can't walk far, but don't do the things I can do with my son. I realised I had no aims any more. So, I asked my son to write down something I could do with him each day and now we play cards, read, draw and paint. I am trying to rest after lunch every day so I can go out some evenings. I have signed up to Twitter, Facebook and have a blog so feel like I have 100 new friends. I am starting an online Latin course in the summer. I feel more like me again and not just an MS patient.'

Remember the friends who have been fountains in the past. Can you reconnect with a text, call or social media? The smirch will say 'No!' and play you some tunes like: *'They won't even remember you'*, *'Why haven't they been in touch?'* *'They will be too busy'*, *'They won't want to meet someone with problems'*. **Can you ignore it's ramblings and do it anyway?**

Chapter 8: Personal Revenge Plan

How small is your smirch?

Can you see the things you could do to shrink the impact your smirch has on you? Just reading this workbook is a bit like reading a diet and exercise book and wondering why your body hasn't changed.

Shrinking your smirch will require putting into practice the shrinking tips and making some changes that will take you closer to who you want to be.

This last chapter will help you decide what to do differently so that the impact of your smirch is as small as it can be.

Let the shrinking begin...

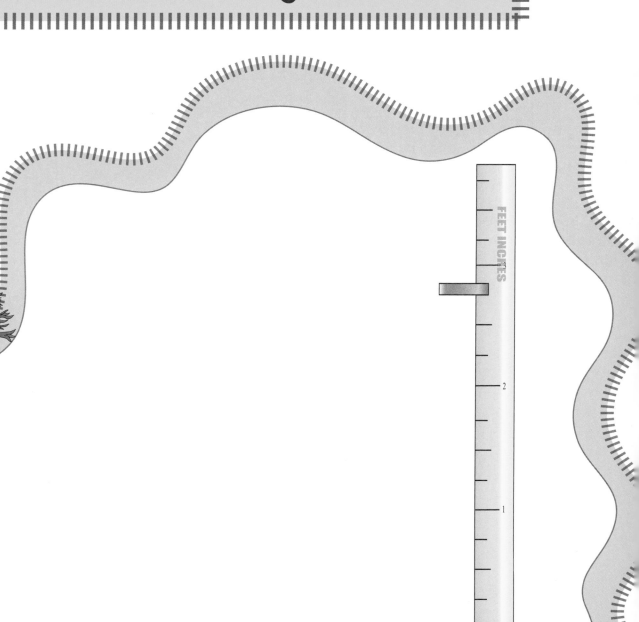

Put here a happy photo of yourself and draw a very small smirch quaking in the corner. He is still there but on your 'struggle days' remind yourself your bag is bigger.

YOUR shrinking section

1

What do I want to be like? What are my values? What things am I going to do however I feel?

....
....
....
....

2

What am I doing too much?

....
....
....
....
....
....

3

What am I not doing enough?

....
....
....
....
....

4

Have I bought a cheerful journal and pen? Add sections for SMART goals, food, mood, pain and movement.

....
....
....
....

5

When am I going to practise noticing, belly breaths, stabilising and connecting? (Now be small, coward!)

....
....
....
....
....

6

What are my smirch's top five tunes? When is the smirchipod on at top volume? What techniques work best to manage my thoughts?

....
....
....
....

7

What feelings do I struggle with most? When do these feelings come up the most often? What techniques can I use to cope better with my feelings?

....
....
....

8 What are my cognitive weaknesses, eg memory, concentration? What strategies can I use to help? When am I going to plan and reflect on my day? ....
....
....
....

9 Write a list of some problems and practise using a problem-solving template.
....
....
....
....

10 How and when am I going to move more? Can I set a SMART goal to help?
....
....
....

11 What do I put in my body that makes it feel better or worse? Can I set a SMART goal to make a small step forward?
....
....
....

12 Do I experience pain? What are the patterns? Can I set a SMART goal to help? Do I need specialist help?
....
....
....

13 What are my energy and fatigue patterns? How do my thoughts, feelings and actions change these patterns? Can I set a SMART goal to manage better my fatigue?
....
....
....

14 When do I rest? What is my personal and family plan to rest more frequently? Would a SMART goal help?
....
....
....

15 Who do I need to get in my shrinking gang? What help do I need?
....
....
....

16 Is there any treasure to be found? Have I learnt anything new from my pain, gained any relationships, improved my outlook?
....
....

17 How can I become more grateful? Start a gratitude diary.
....
....

Draw a picture of [y]our large resource bag with all the [to]ols you think could [b]e useful and put [it] with your speech [a]bout who you want to be.

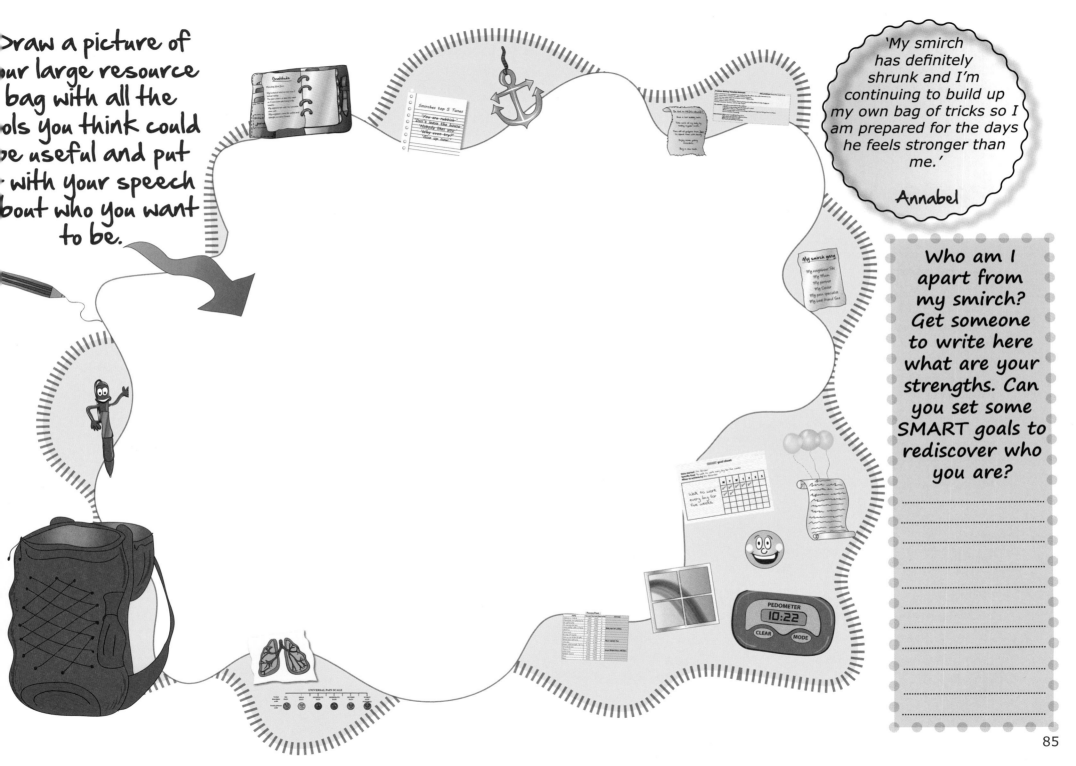

Who am I apart from my smirch? Get someone to write here what are your strengths. Can you set some SMART goals to rediscover who you are?

....
....
....
....
....
....
....
....
....
....
....

Books

Mental health

The Overcoming Series
Various authors
Self-help guides using cognitive behavioural techniques for many different mental health issues. These include depression, anxiety, traumatic stress, anxiety, chronic pain, anger and eating disorders.

The reality slap
Russ Harris

Get out of your mind and into your life
Steven C Hayes

Mindfulness for dummies
Shamash Alidina

Neurological conditions

The stress and mood management program for individuals with MS
David Mohr

Head injury
Trevor Powell

Brain injury survivor guide
Larry and Beth Jameson

Brain injury survival kit
Cheryle Sullivan

For children and young people

My parent has a brain injury
Jo Johnson

Think good—feel good: a CBT workbook for children and young people
Paul Stallard

Some of these references, websites and apps are condition-specific but lots of conditions share symptoms, eg fatigue, pain, cognitive problems and low mood. So it is worth checking out ALL the resources.

Christian-based resources

John MacArthur's Study Bible
John MacArthur

The Message: The Bible in contemporary language
Eugene H. Peterson

Depression: a rescue plan
Jim Winter

Novels

Mr Chartwell
Rebecca Hunt
A novel based on Winston Churchhill's black dog

Websites

Neurological conditions

Headway
www.headway.org.uk

Shift MS
www.shift.ms/

www.mstrust.org
Staying Smart
www.stayingsmart.org.uk

Multiple Sclerosis Society
www.mssociety.org.uk

Dementia UK
www.dementiauk.org

Alzheimer's Society
www.alzheimers.org.uk

Brain Injury Rehabilitation Trust
www.thedtgroup.org/brain-injury

Parkinson's Disease Society
www.parkinsons.org.uk

Different Strokes
www.differentstrokes.co.uk

Stroke Association
www.stroke.org.uk

European Parkinson's Disease Association
www.epda.eu.com

Epilepsy Society
www.epilepsysociety.org.uk

Mental health

SANE
www.sane.org.uk

For self-help
www.getselfhelp.co.uk
www.psychologytools.org

Samaritans
www.samaritans.org

Mind
www.mind.org.uk

Northumberland, Tyne and Wear self help
www.ntw.nhs.uk

Living Life to the Full
www.lttf.com

Young people

Action for Children
www.actionforchildren.org.uk

The Children's Society
www.childrenssociety.org.uk

The Prince's Trust
www.princes-trust.org.uk

Carers Trust
www.youngcarers.net

Childline
www.childline.org.uk

Bereavement

Winston's Wish
www.winstonswish.org.uk

Cruse Bereavement Care
www.cruse.org.uk

WAY Widowed Young

www.wayfoundation.org.uk

Join the shrinking gang on Facebook!
https://www.facebook.com/shrinkingthesmirch

Useful apps

Friends with Mindi	Moodtracker	Anxiety
SMART goals	Moodkit	Beat panic
Headspace	Moodmaster	Moody me
Being still	eCBTmood	Mood panda
	eCBTtrauma	Breathe2relax
	eCBTanger	Befoodsmart
	eCBTeating	PsychMeUp

The smirch-defeating team are:
Jo Johnson (author) Lauren Densham (illustrator)
Graham Thrussell (proof-reader)

The team **all** believe, that whilst the 20 shrinking tips will improve how you feel about life, the most life-changing smirch-shrinking message is summed up perfectly by Tim Keller in his book *The Reason for God*.
He says: 'The only true answer to life's struggles is in the Christian gospel, which is that; I am so flawed that Jesus had to die for me, yet I am so loved and valued that Jesus was glad to die for me.'
The New Testament book of John, found in the Bible, is a good place to start if you want more information.

Happy shrinking!